For Peggy and Rufus.

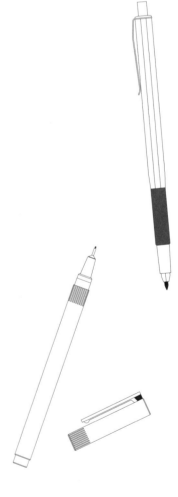

An Allocated Space production
www.allocatedspace.com

Published in 2008 by Laurence King Publishing Ltd
361–373 City Road, London EC1V 1LR
United Kingdom
T +44 (0)20 7841 6900
F +44 (0)20 7841 6910
enquiries@laurenceking.co.uk
www.laurenceking.co.uk

Copyright © 2008 Mark Boyce
Edited by Lizzy McLean
Designed and illustrated by the author

A catalog record for this book is available from the British Library

ISBN-13: 978-1-85669-543-5

Typeset in Tondo, kindly supplied by Dalton Maag
www.daltonmaag.com

Printed in China

This book references the varying standard
formats and systems used within graphic design.
Part sketchbook, part reference book, and
part notebook, it is a space for composing and
visualizing layouts, sketching and developing
ideas, taking reference, and making note.

Sizes May Vary
A workbook for graphic design
Mark Boyce

*US graph paper has been developed specifically
for graphic design. The rectangles created by
its unique grid have the same aspect ratios as the
American national standard for paper sizes.

How / to / be / a / graphic / designer, / without / losing / your / soul /

Adrian Shaughnessy

Interviews with: Neville Brody, Natalie Hunter, Rudy VanderLans, John Warwicker, Angela Lorenz, Alexander Gelman, Andy Cruz, Kim Hiorthøy, Peter Stemmler, Corey Holms. / Designed by Bibliothèque.

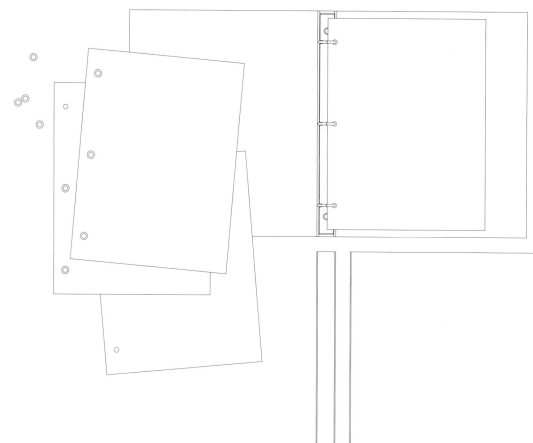

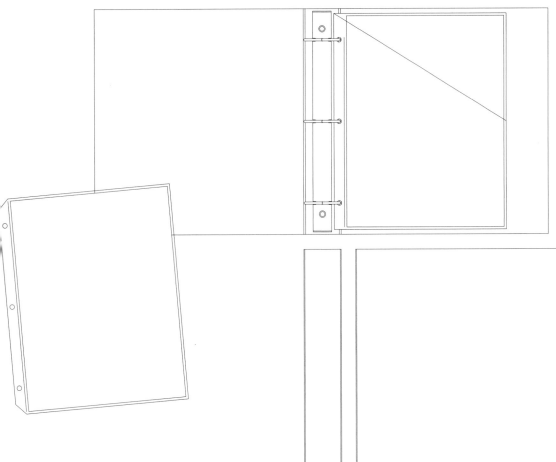

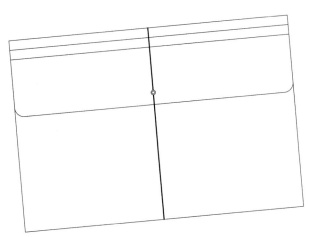

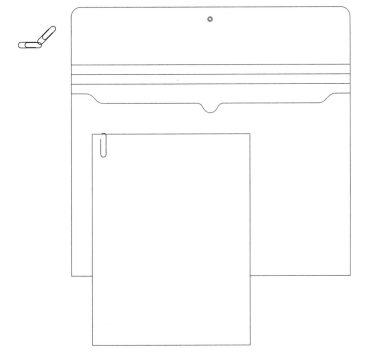

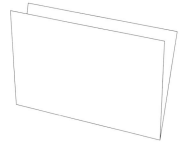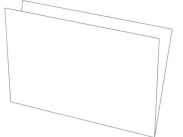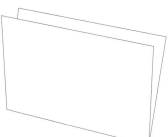
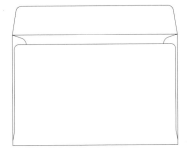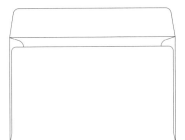

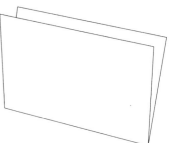
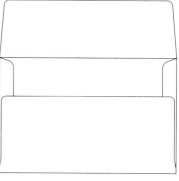
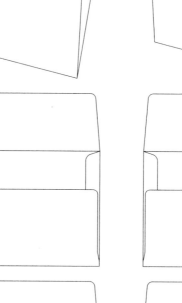

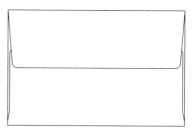

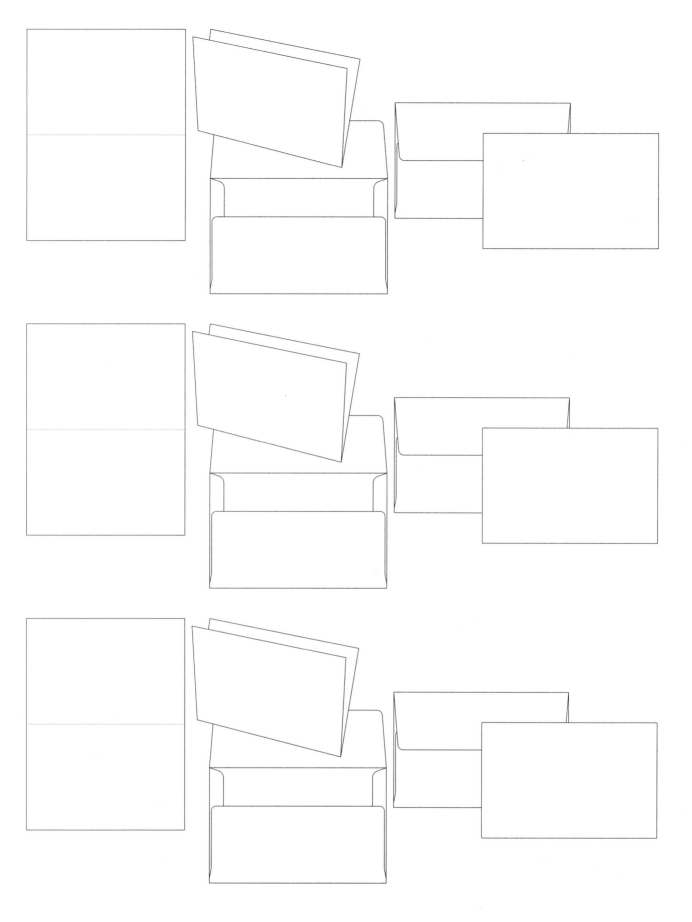

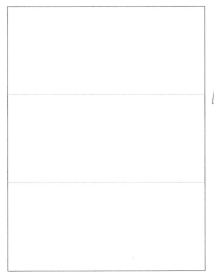

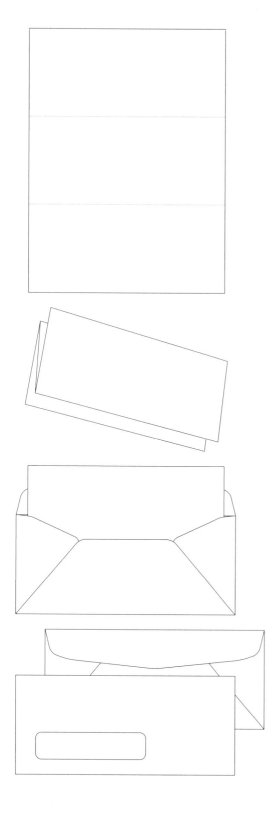

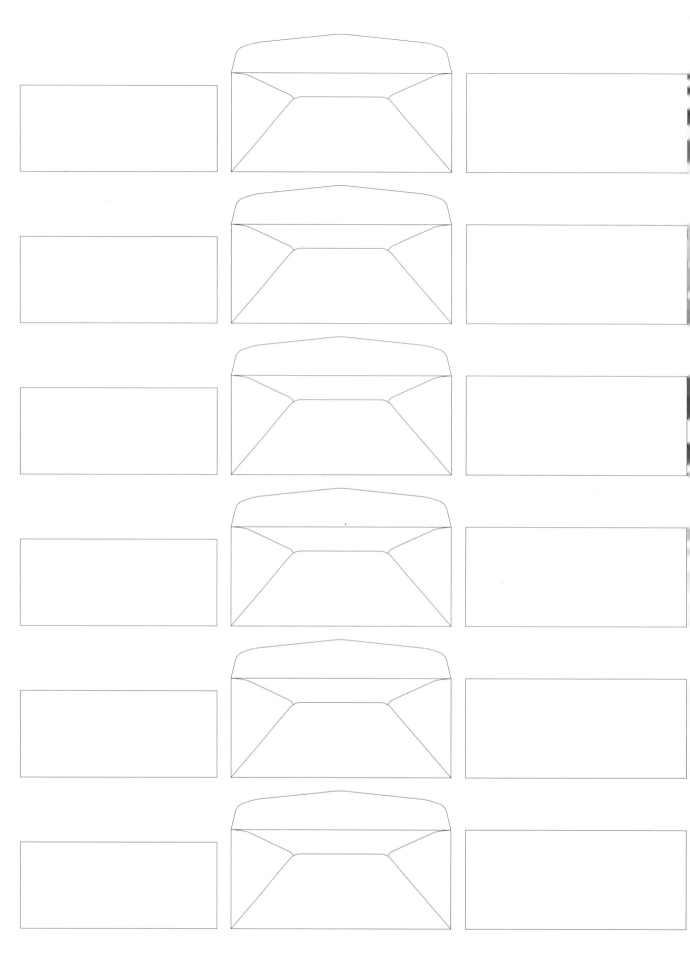

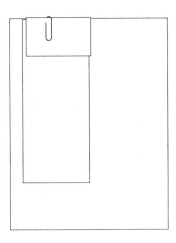

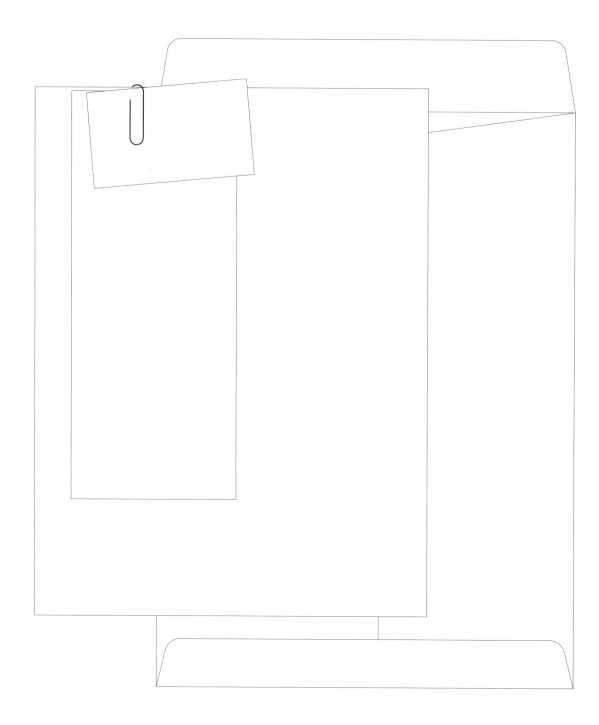

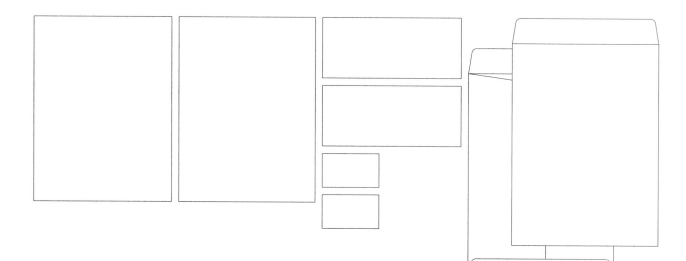

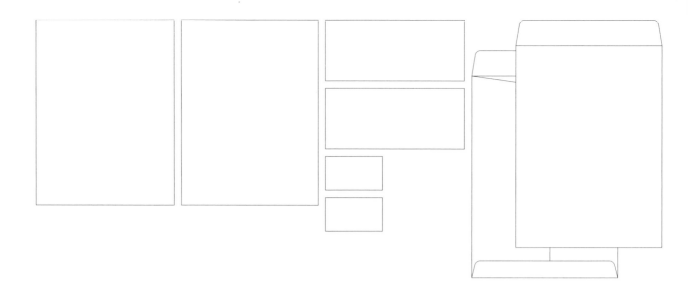

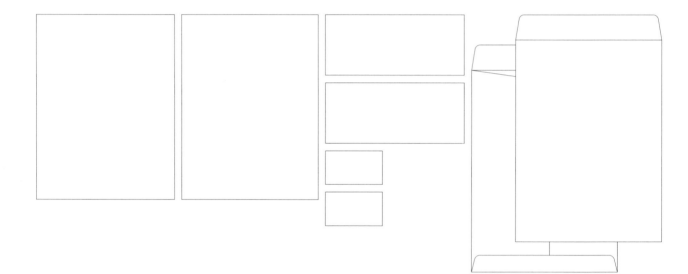

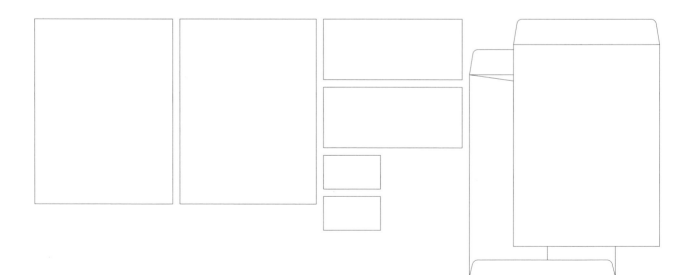

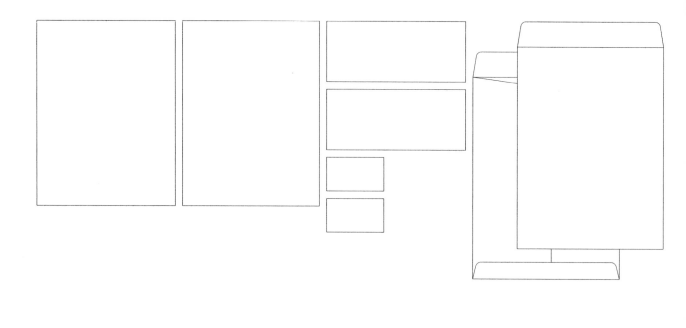

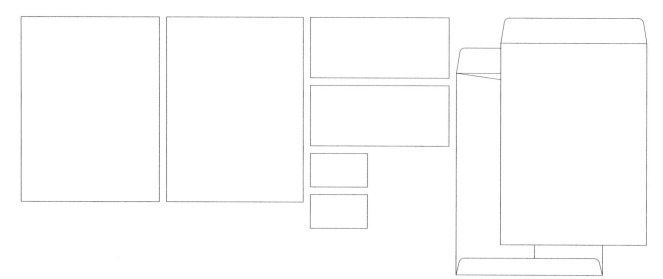

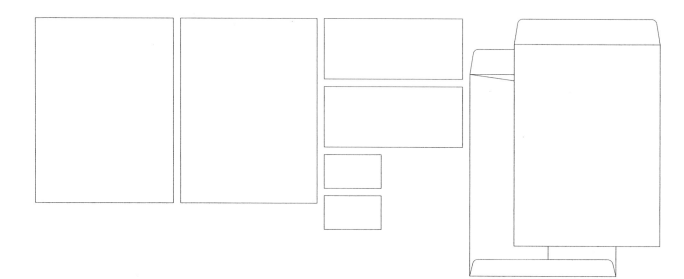

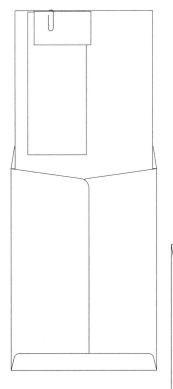
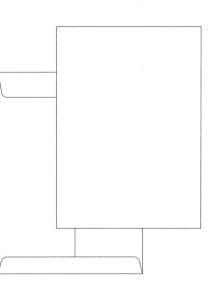

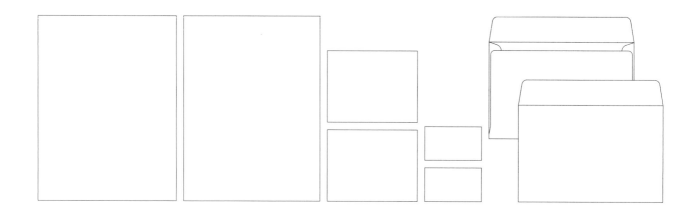

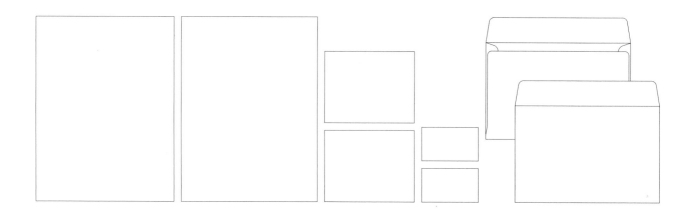

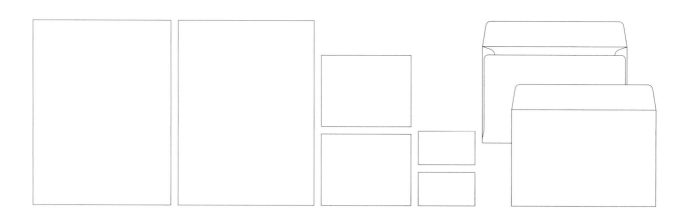

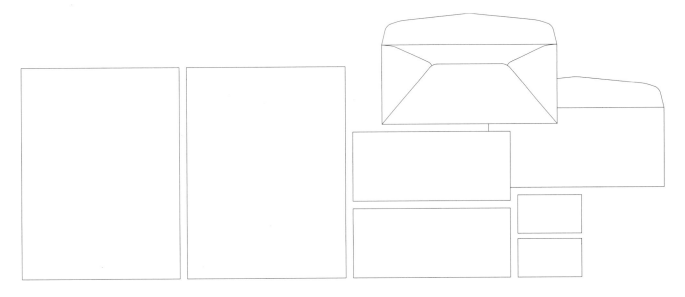

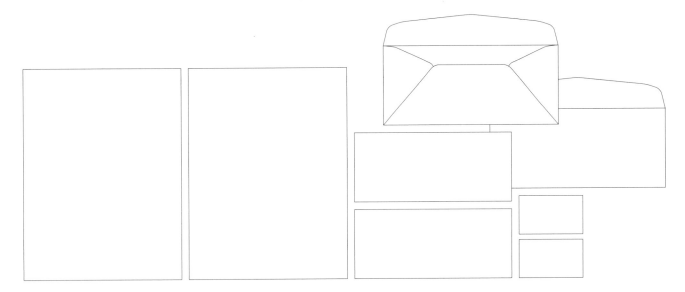

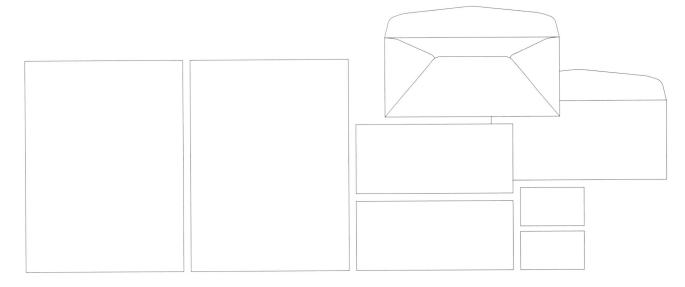

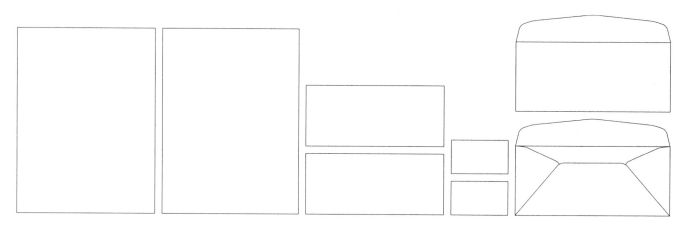

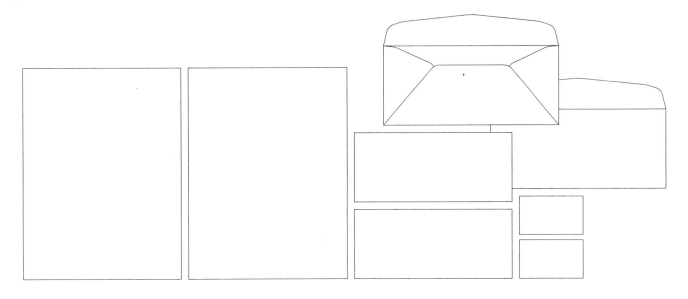

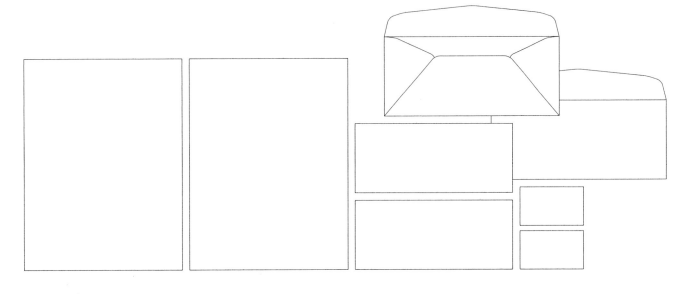

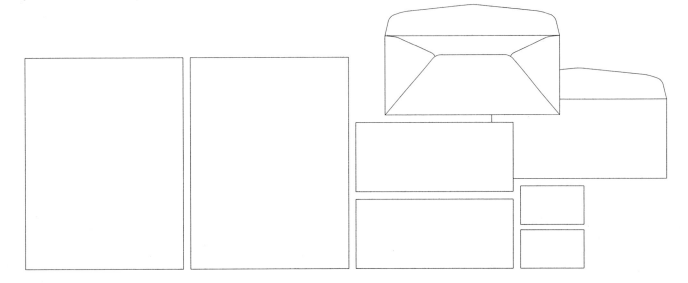

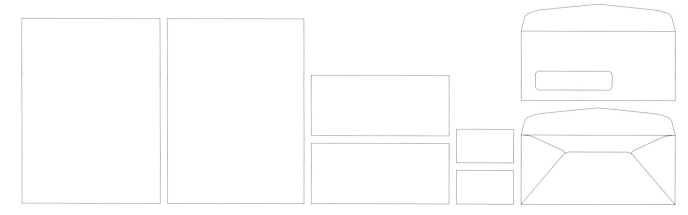

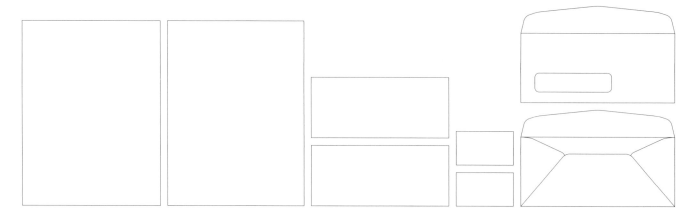

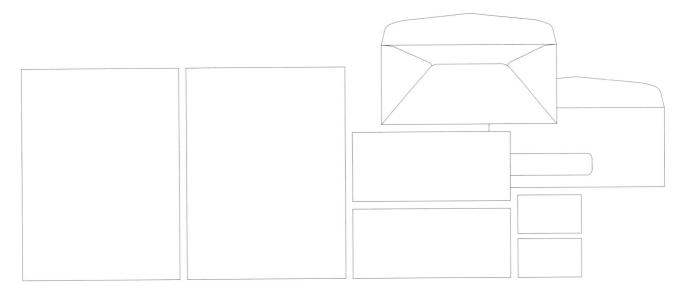

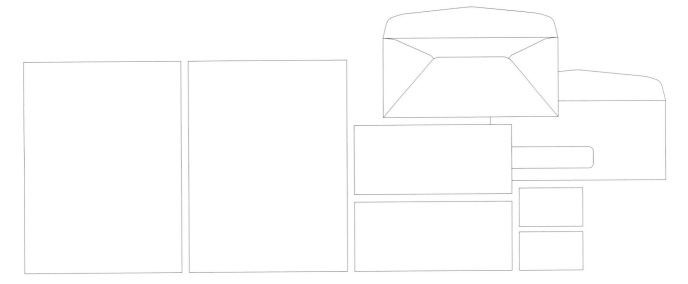

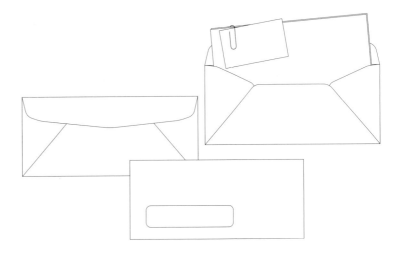

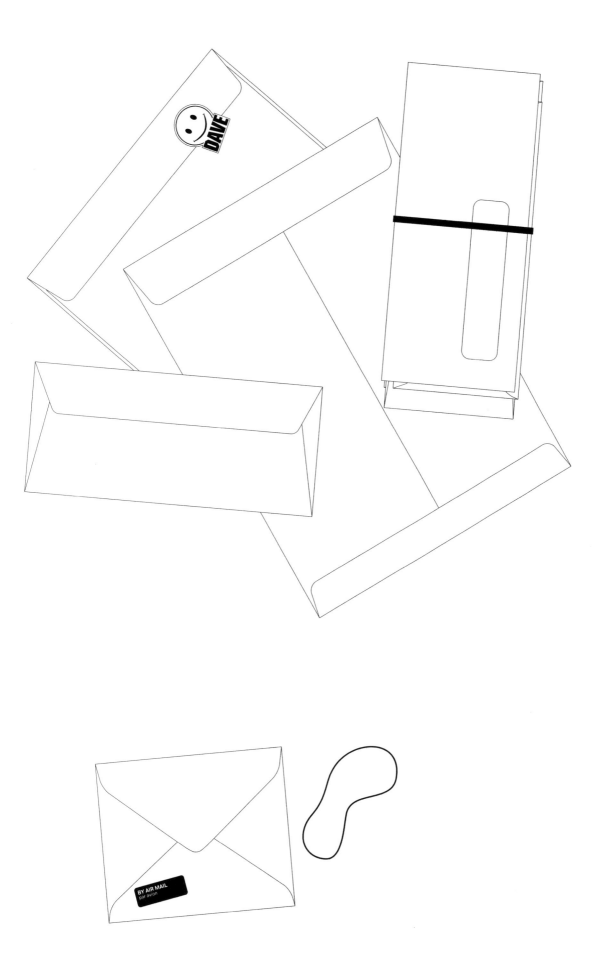

LAURENCE KING

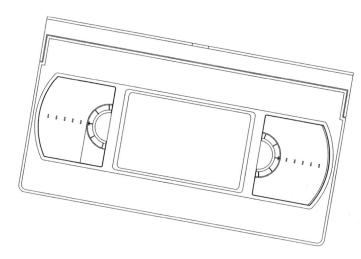

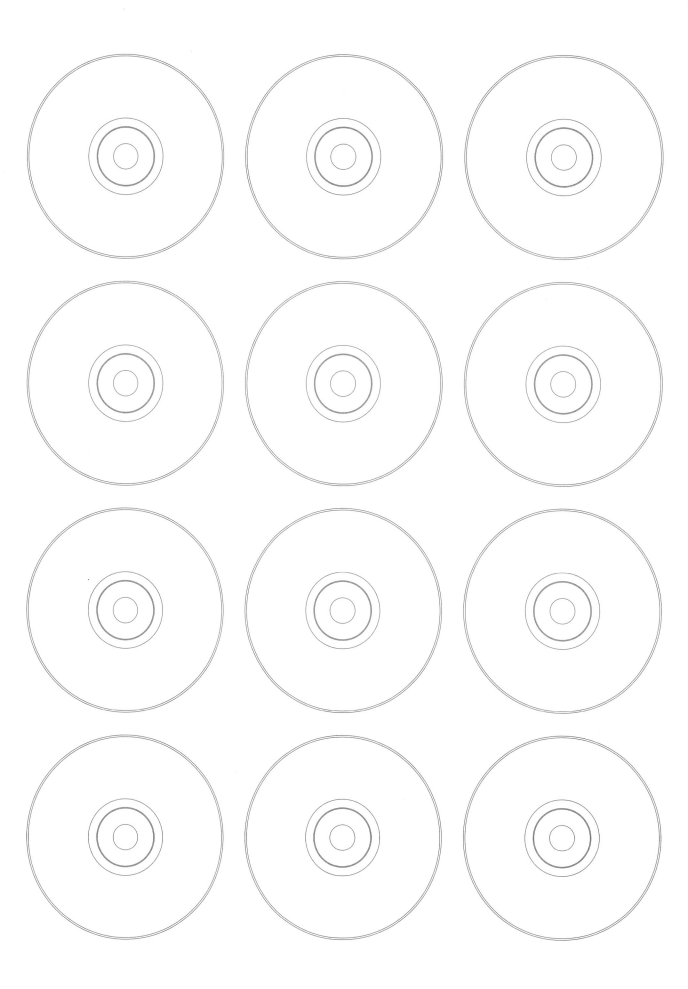

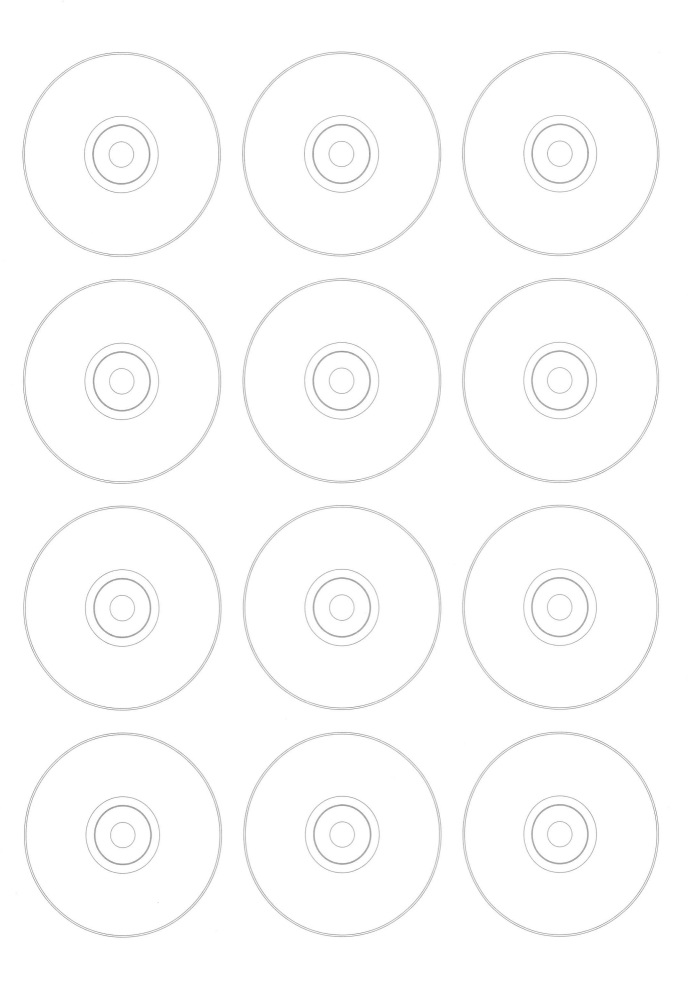

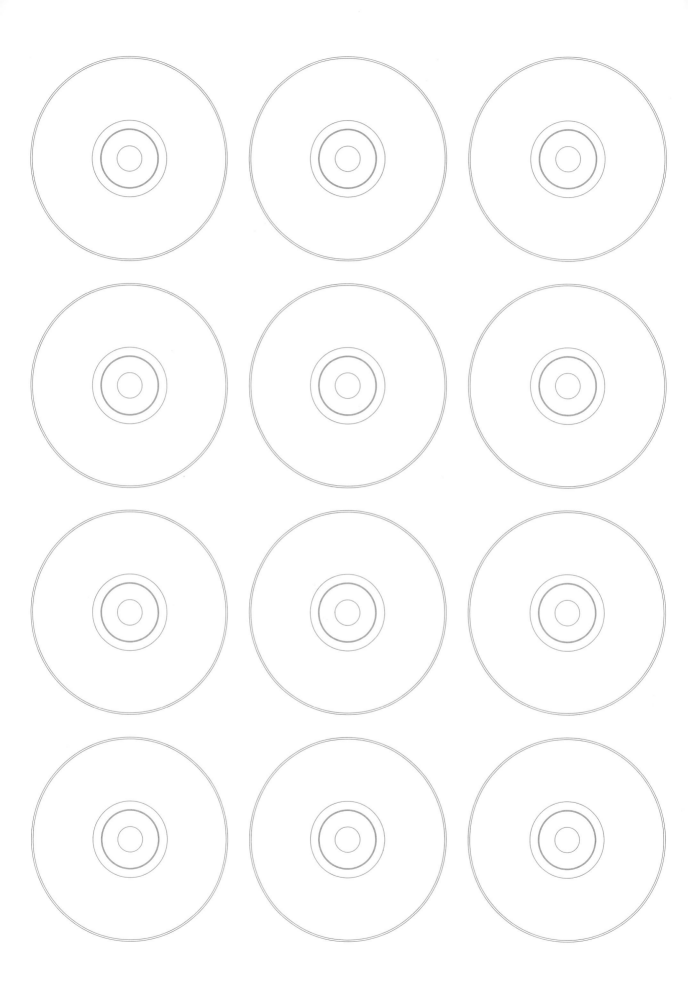

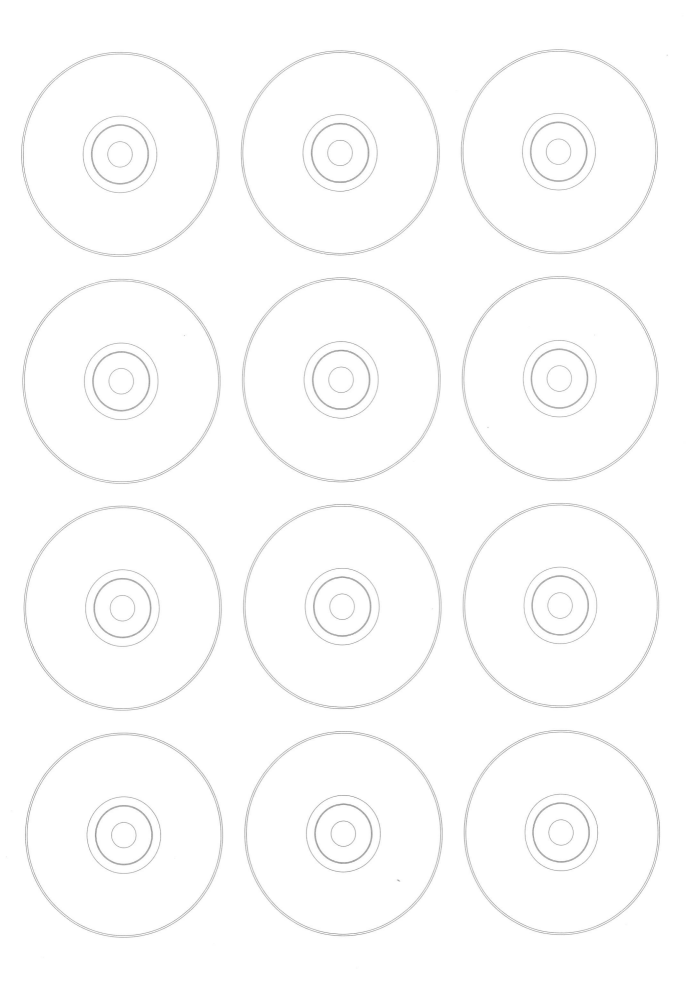

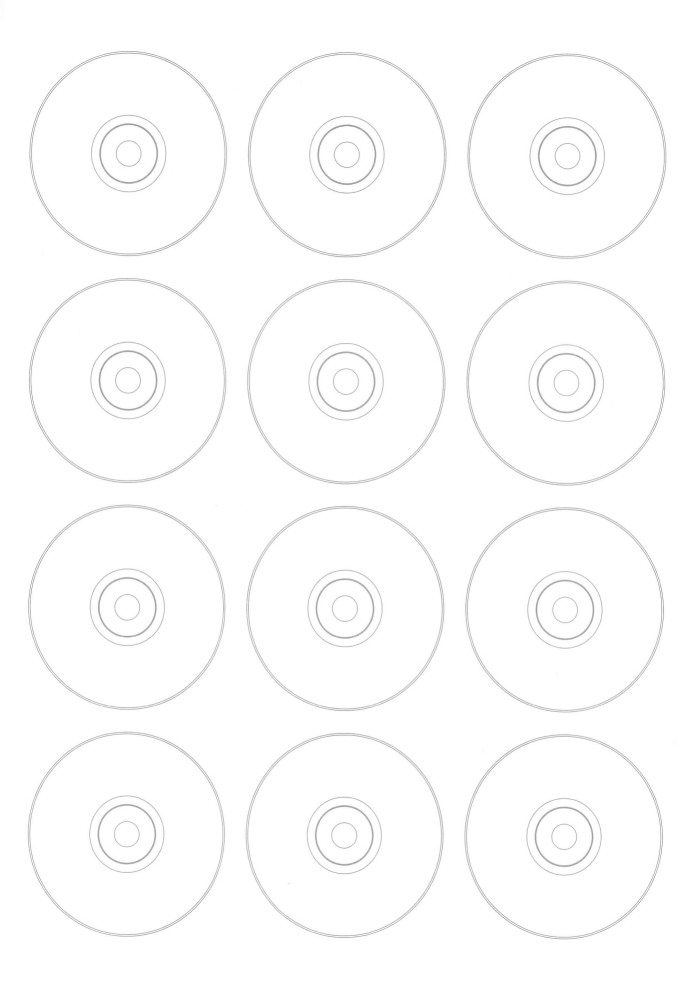

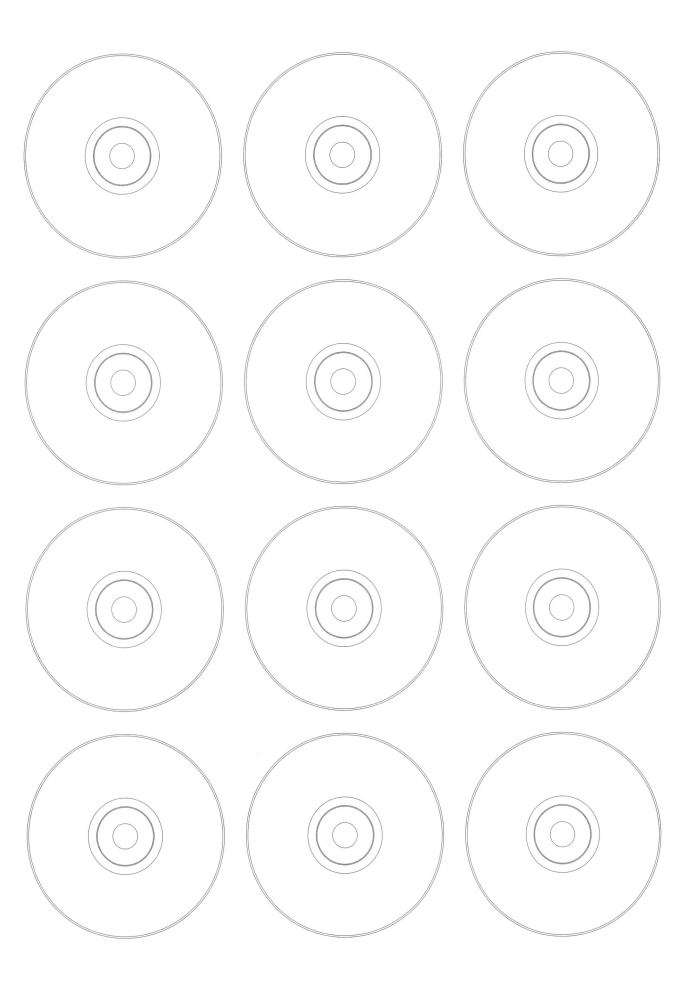

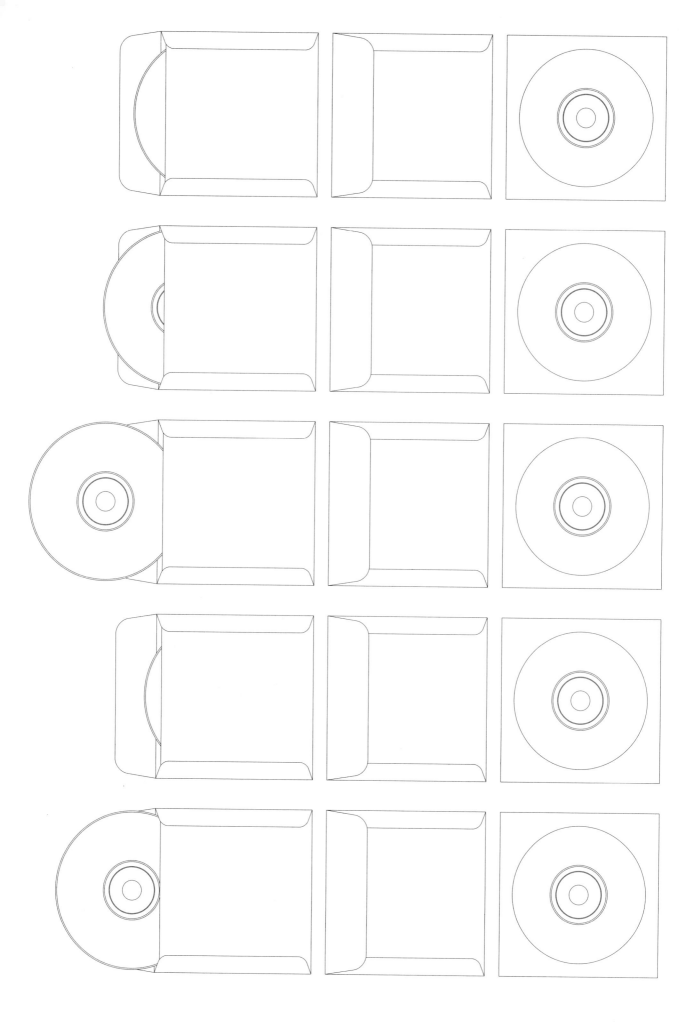

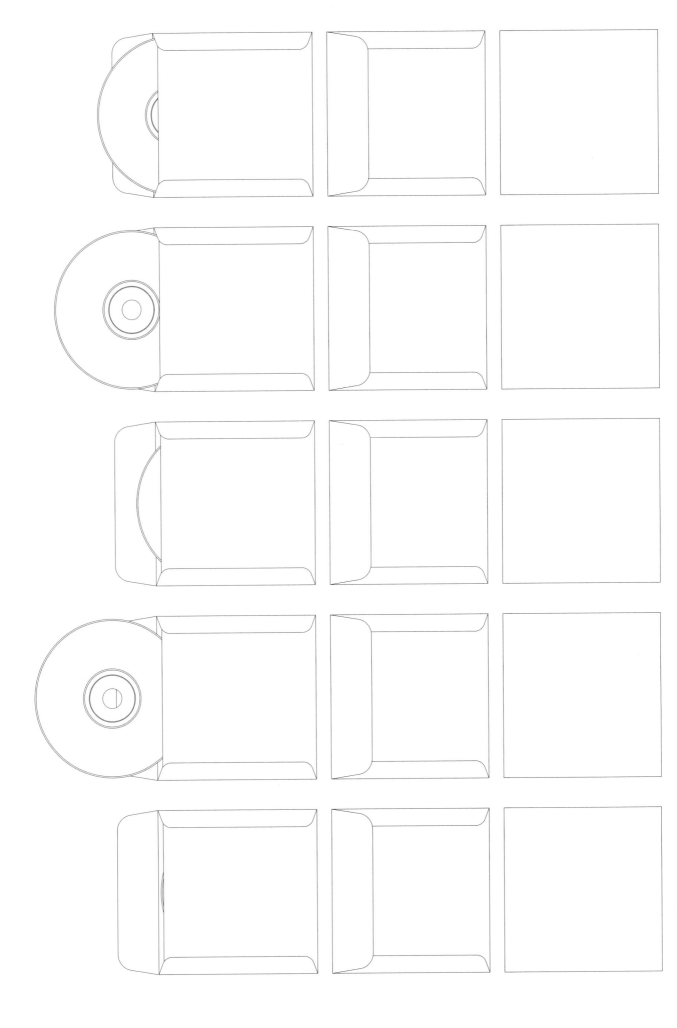

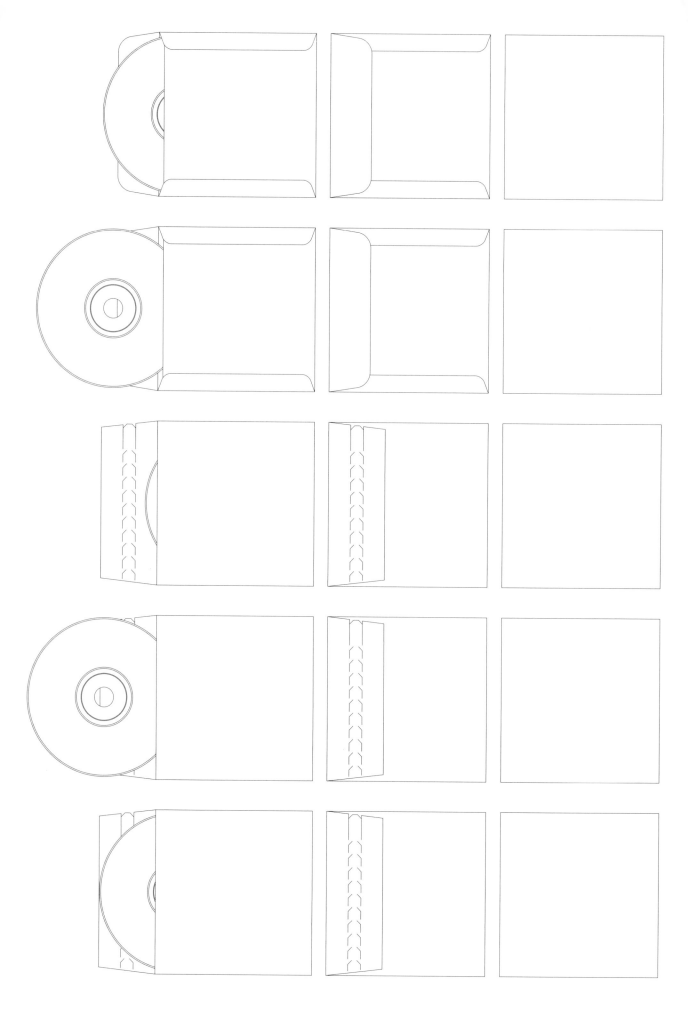

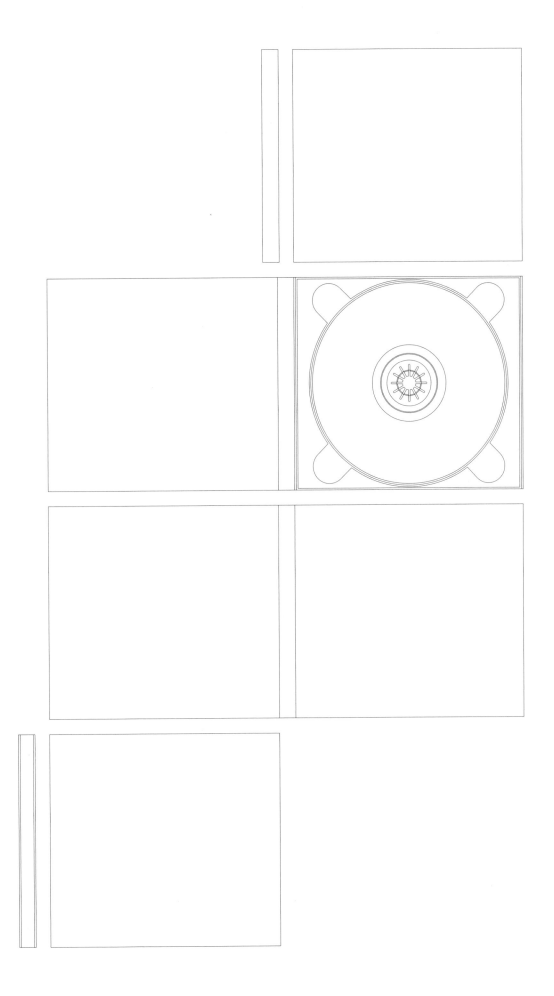

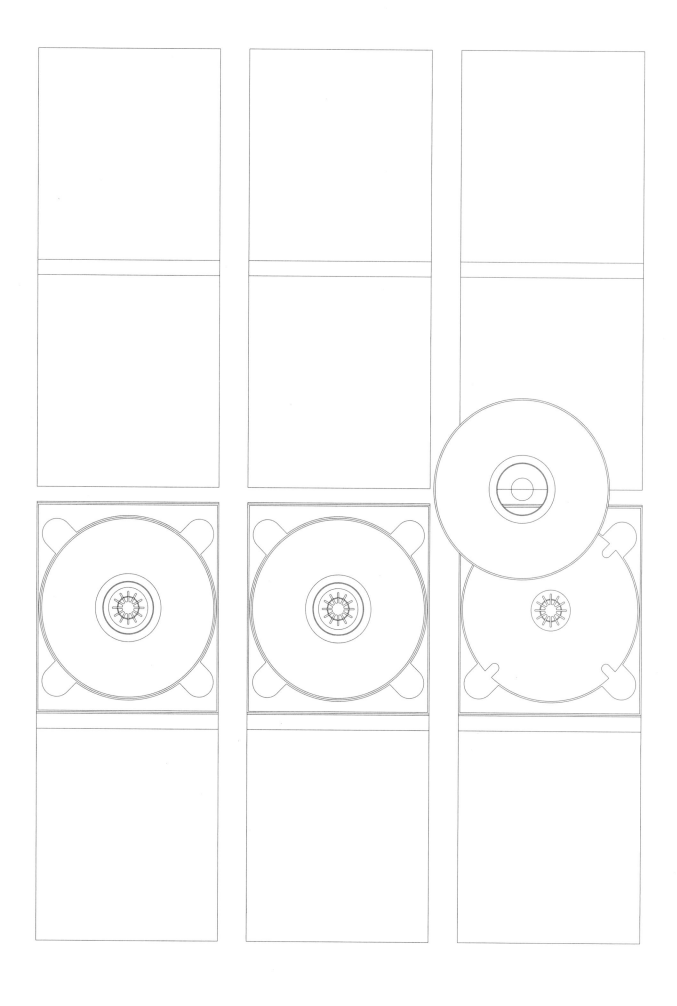

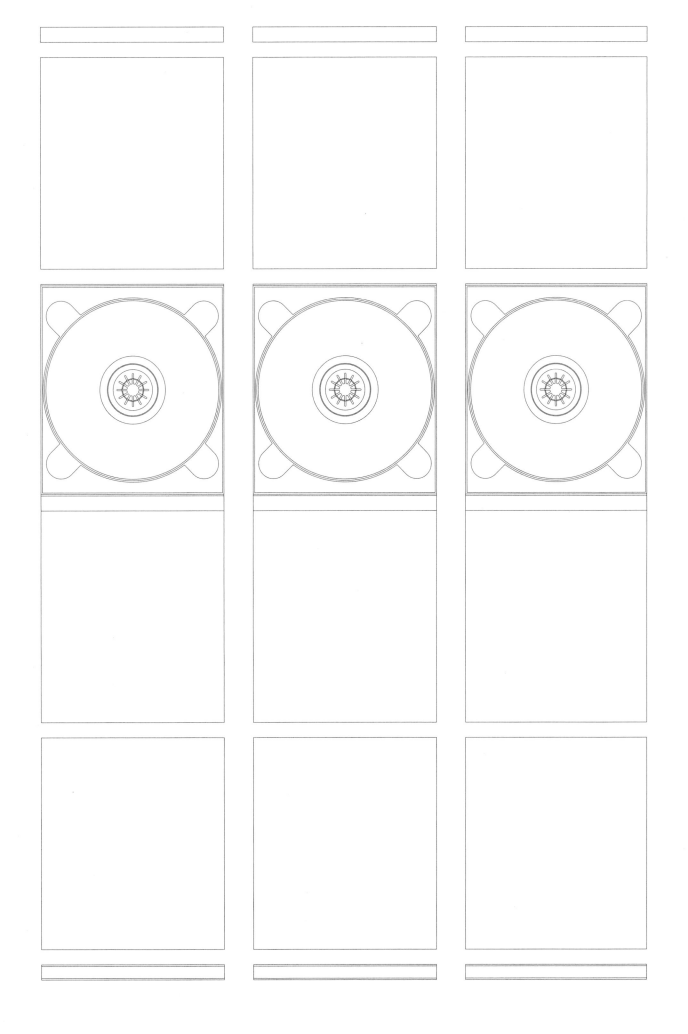

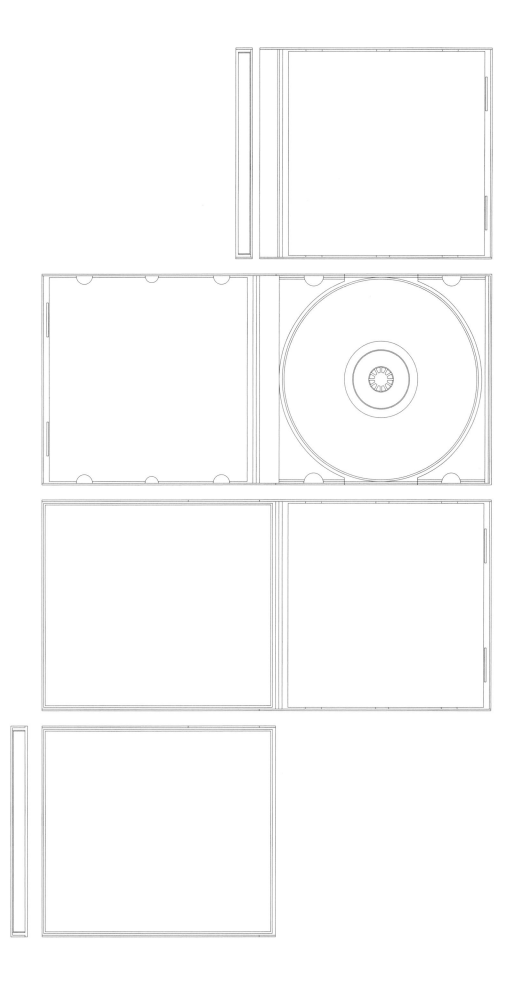

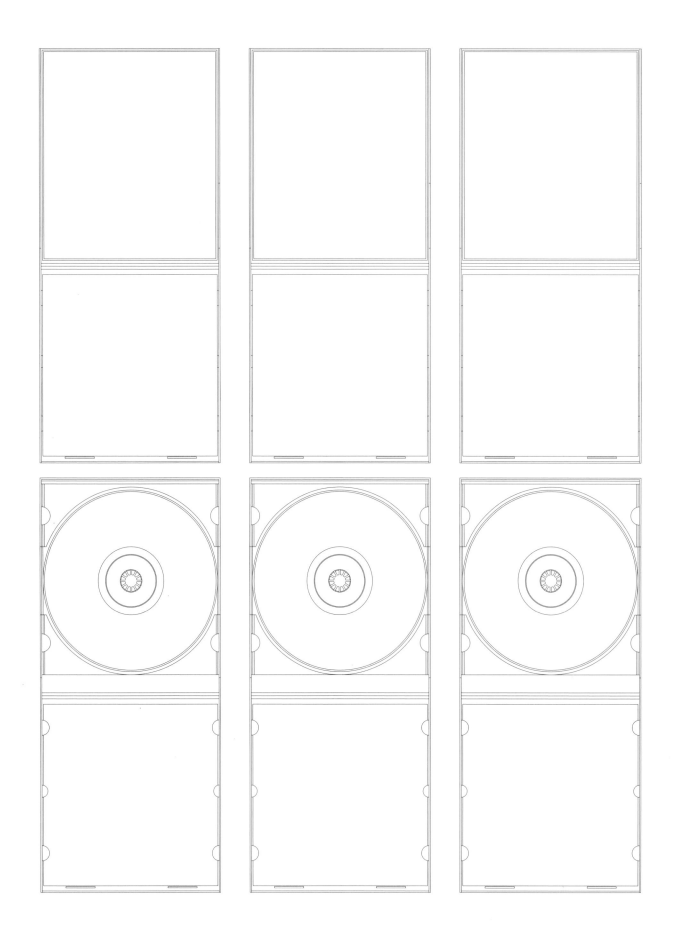

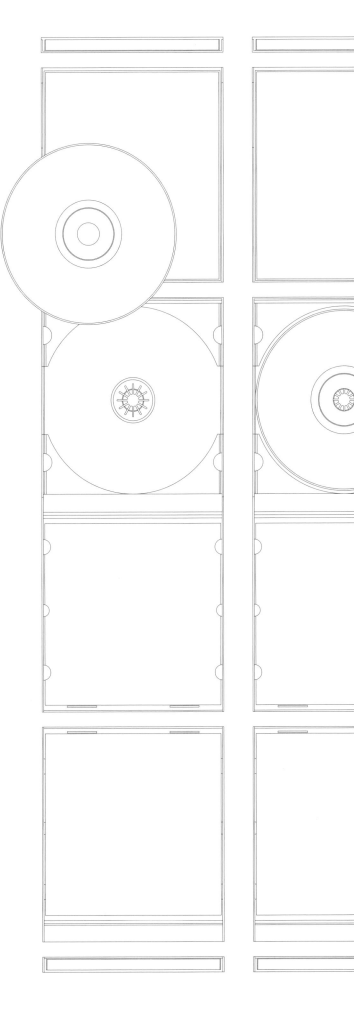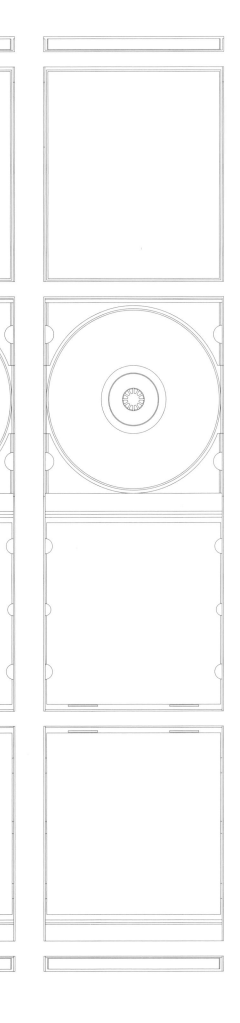

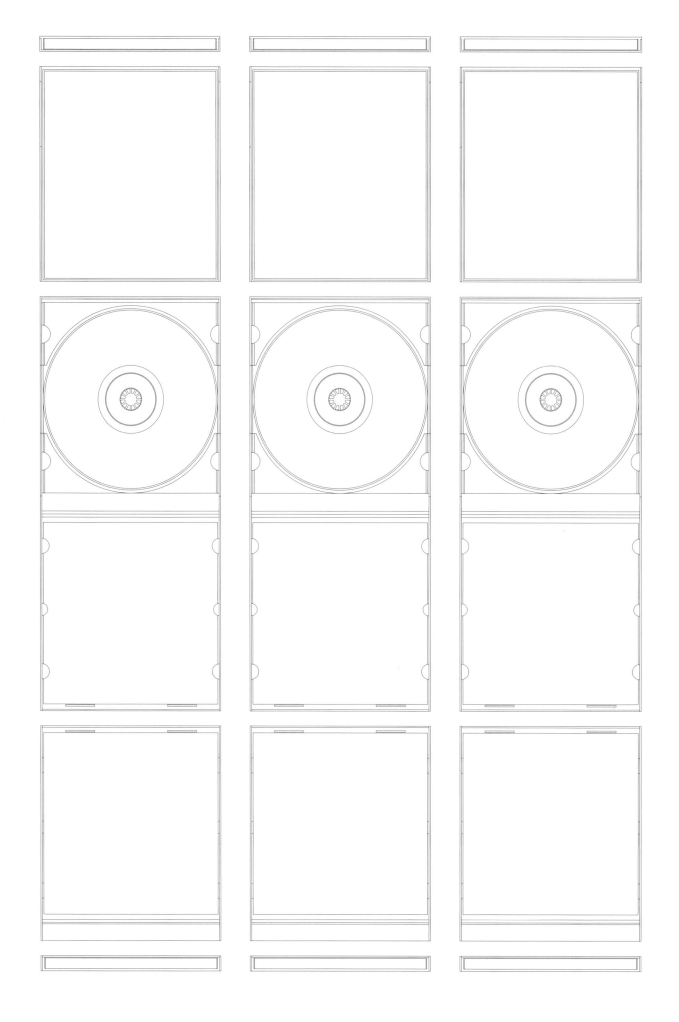

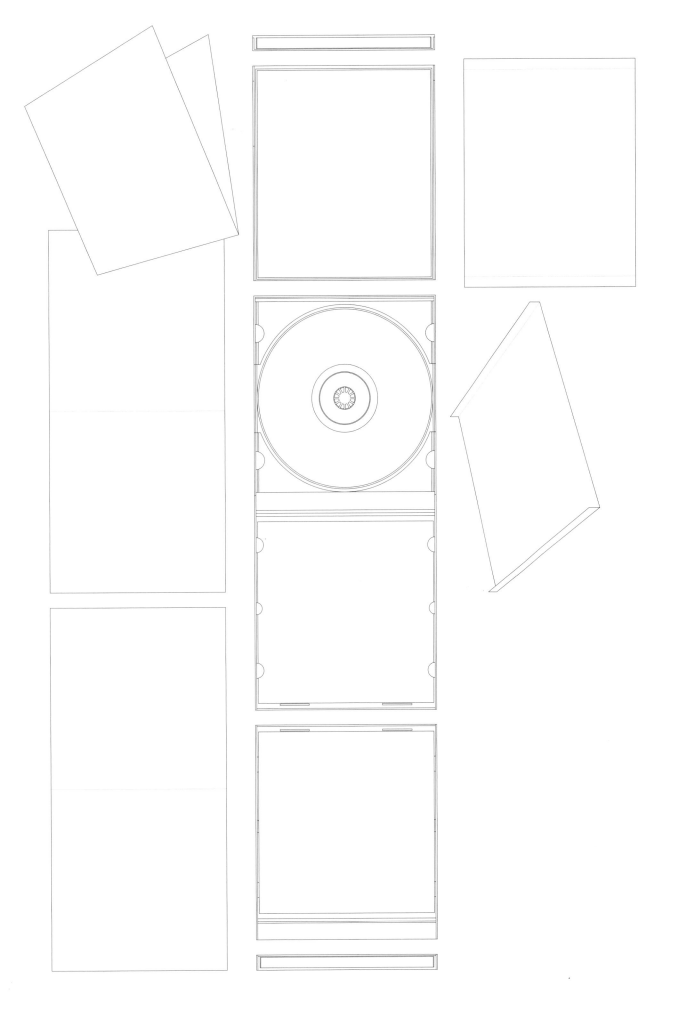

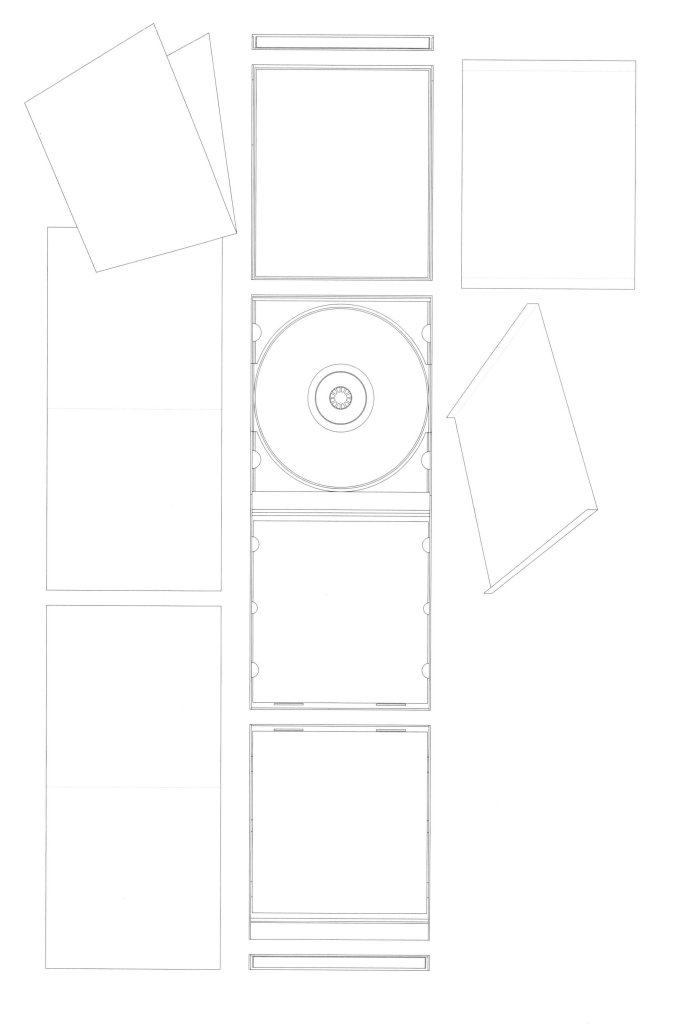

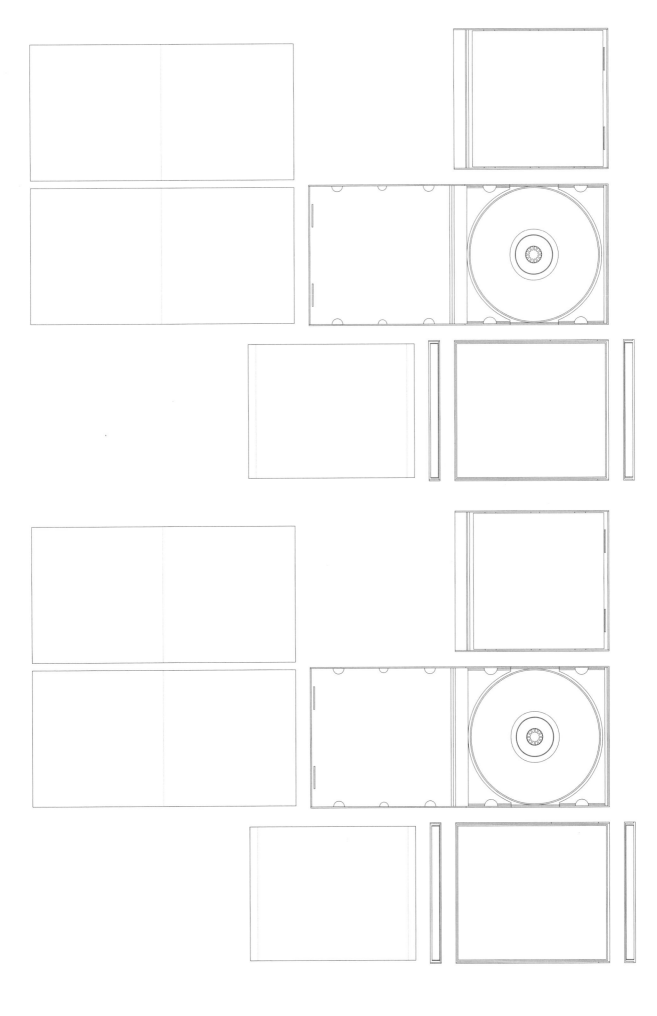

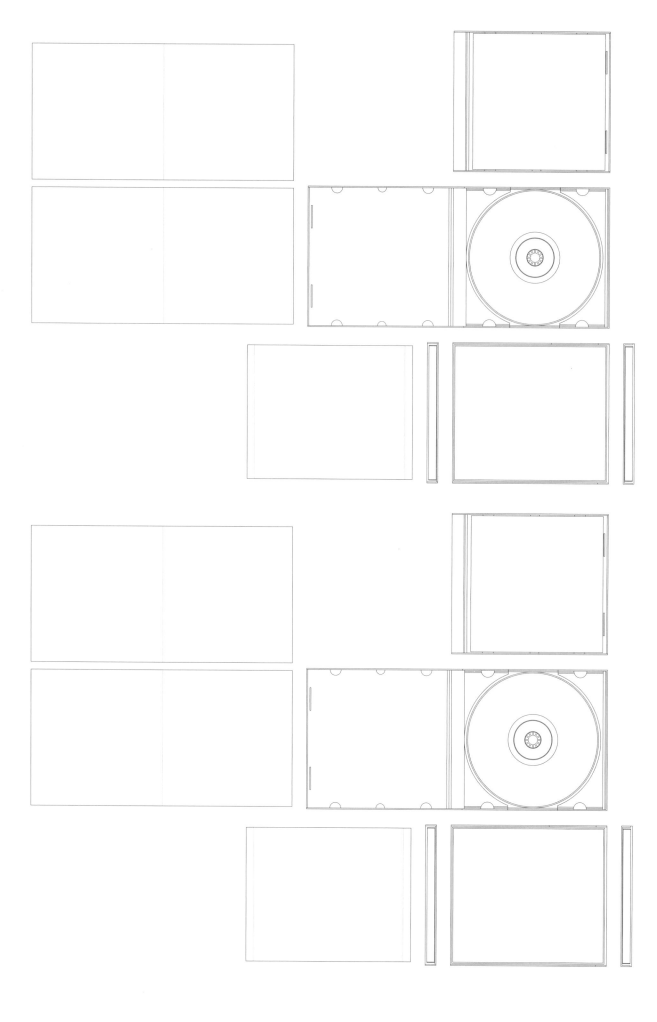

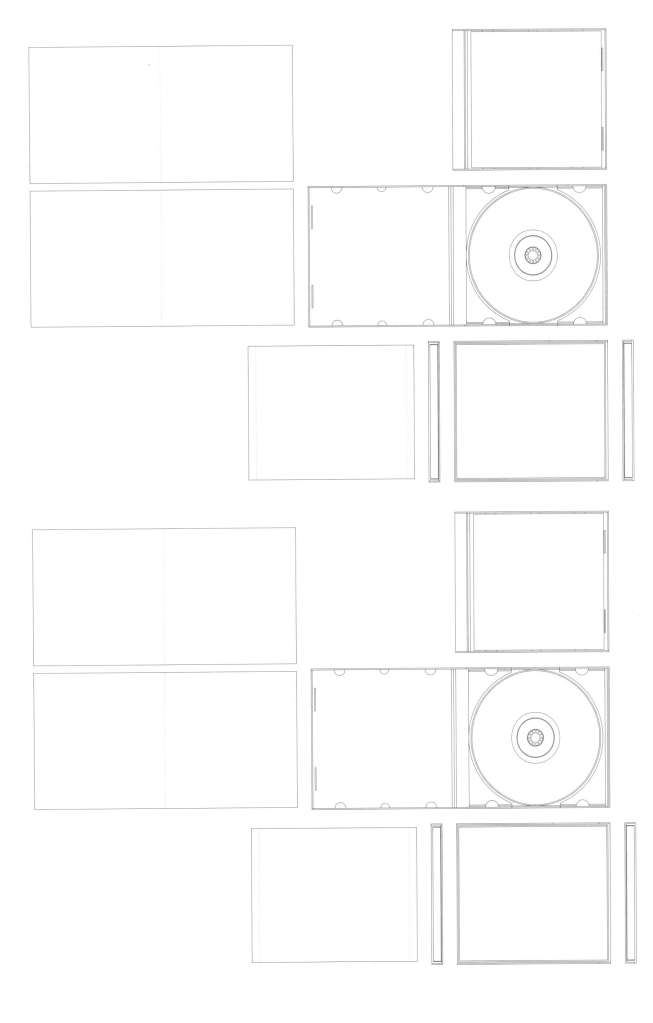

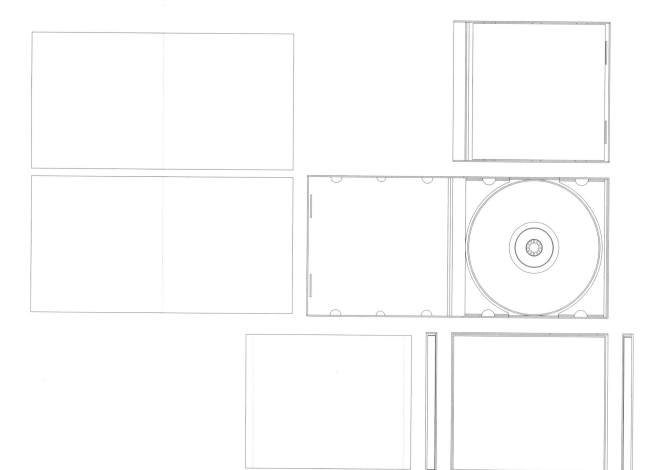
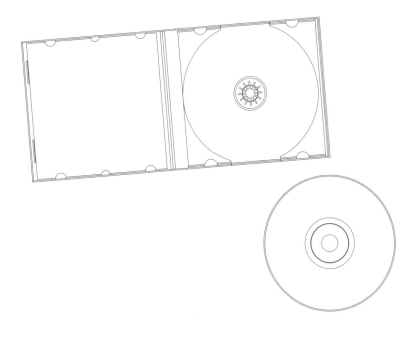

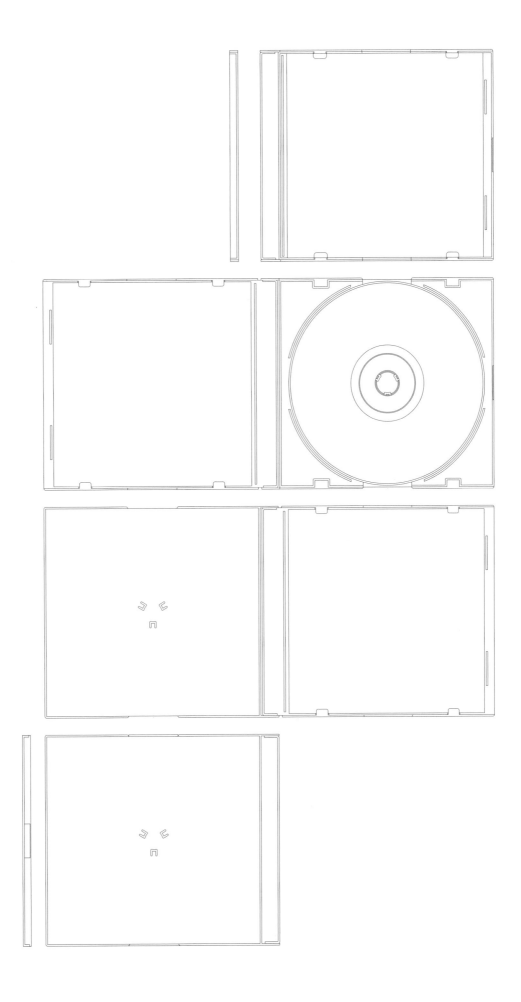

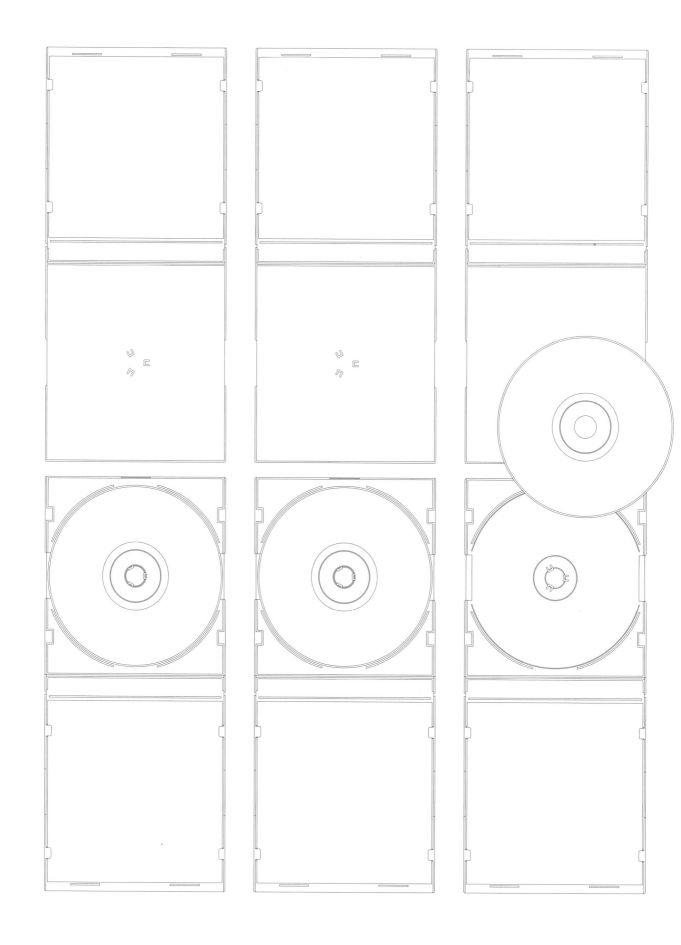

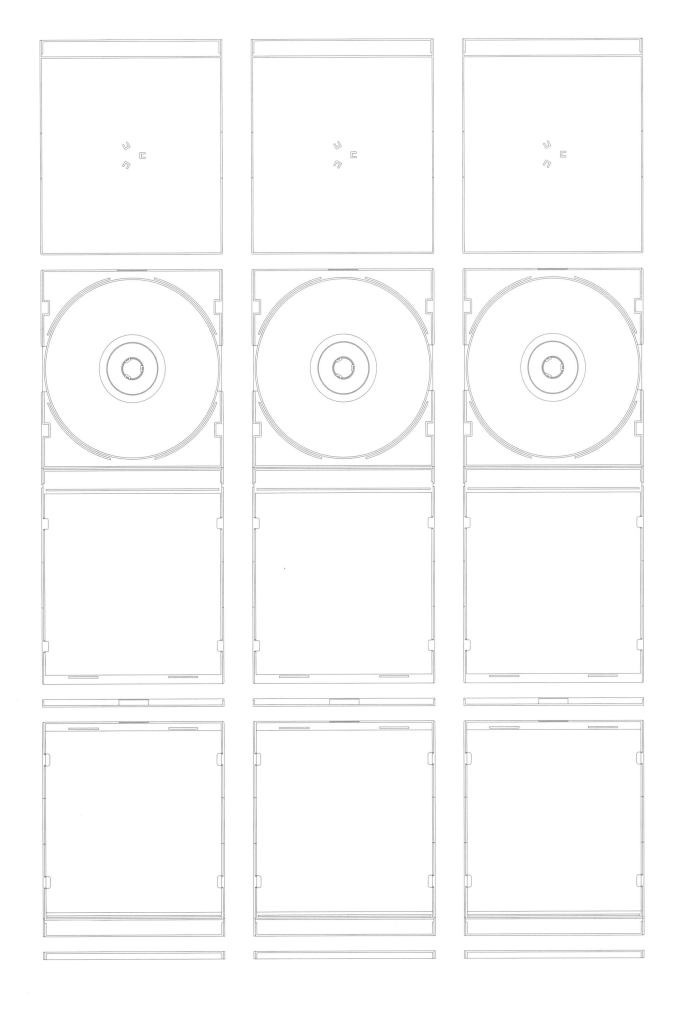

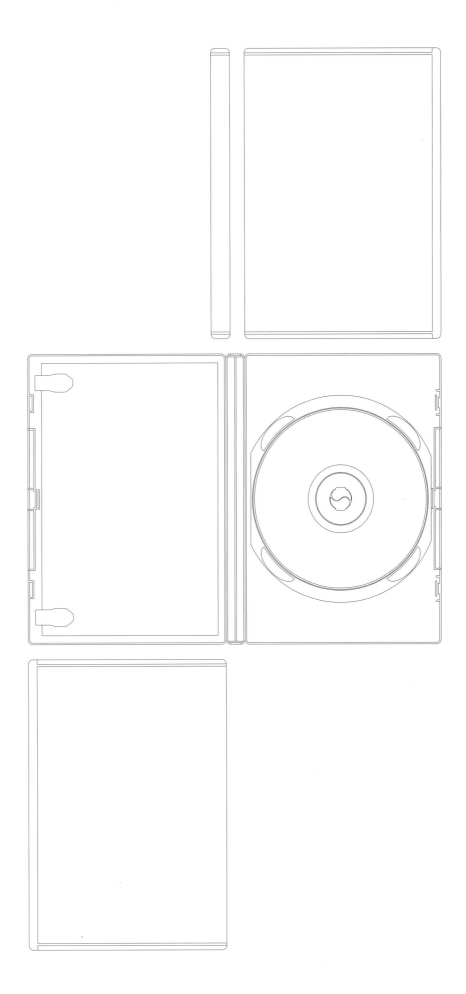

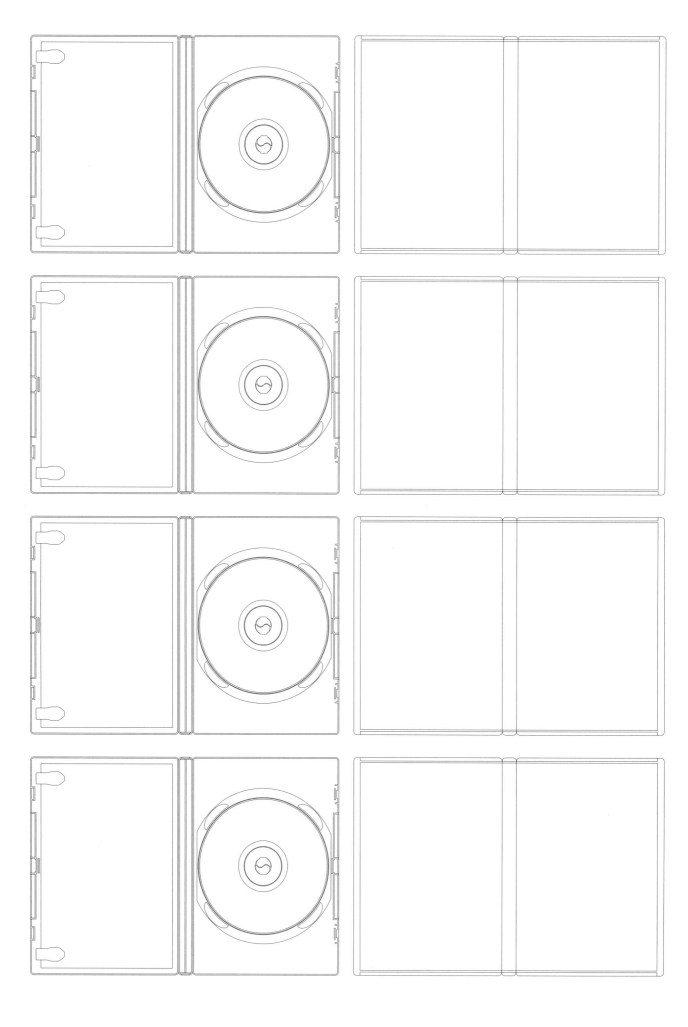

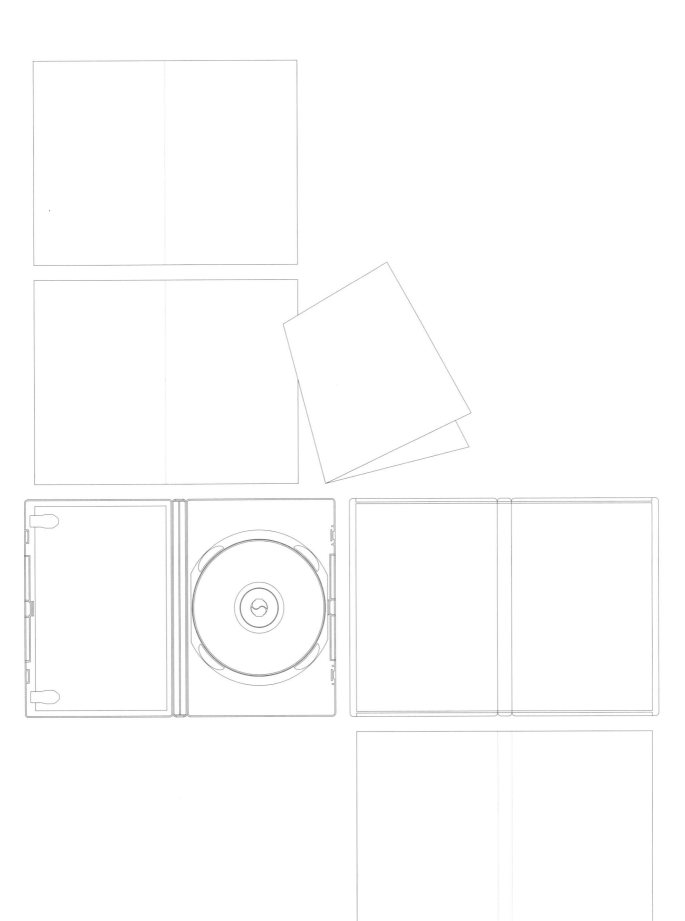

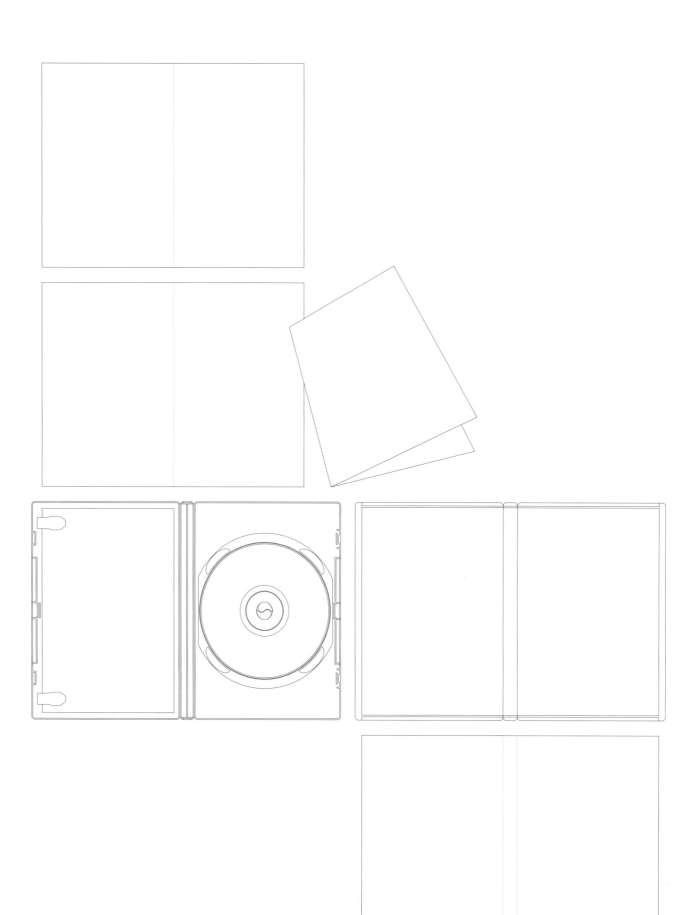

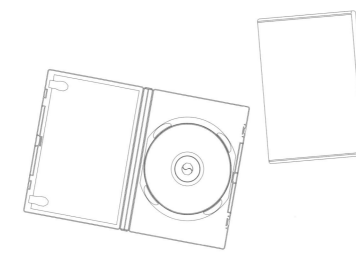

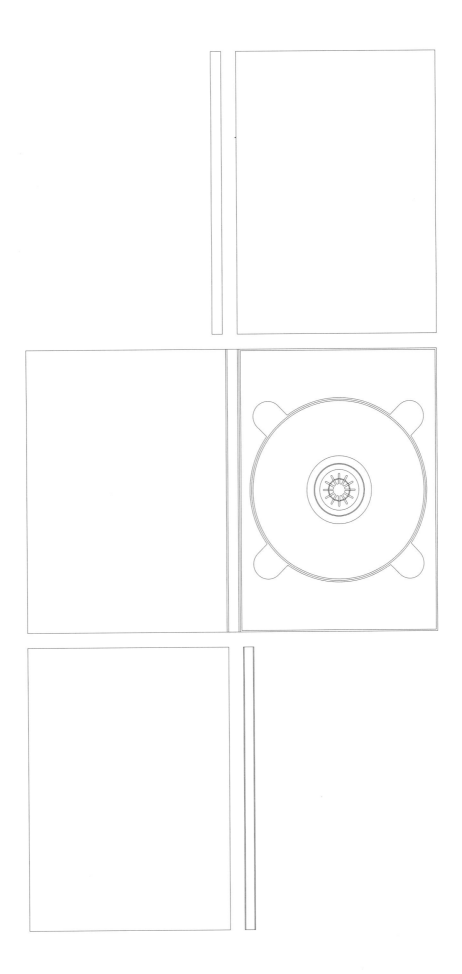

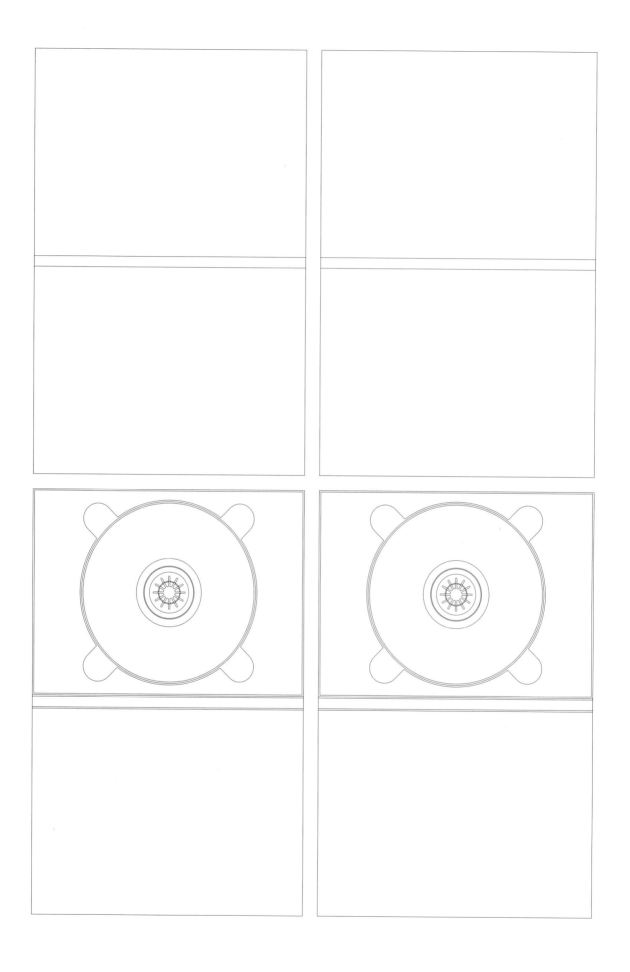

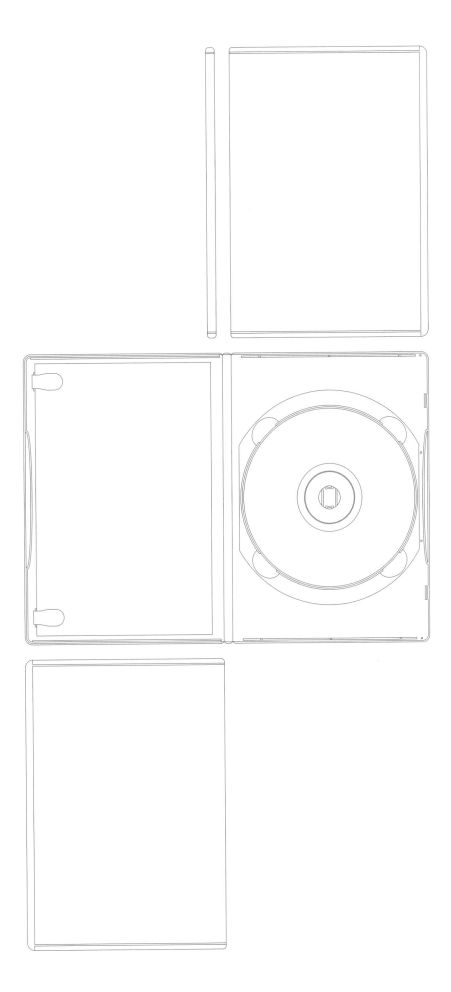

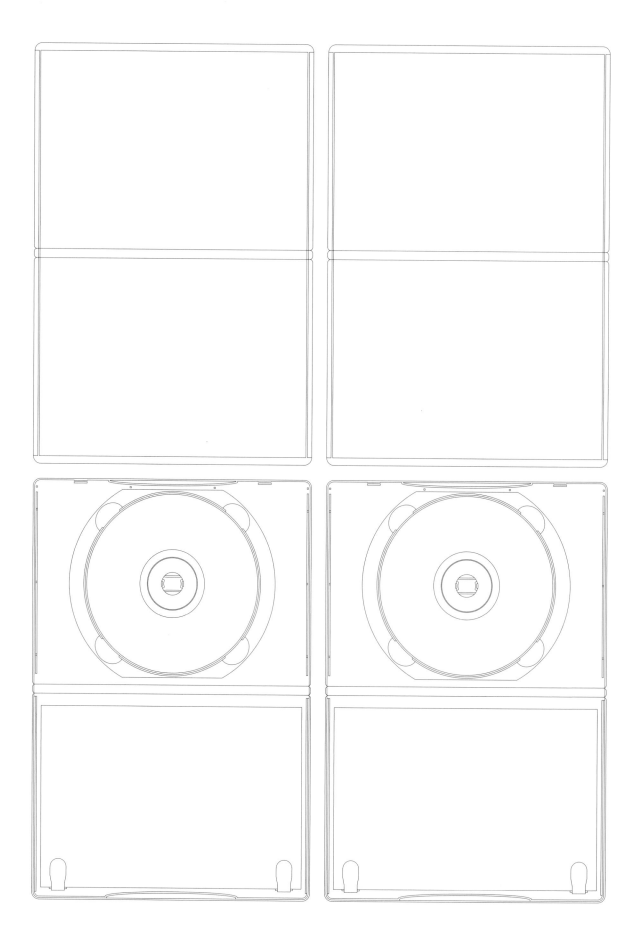

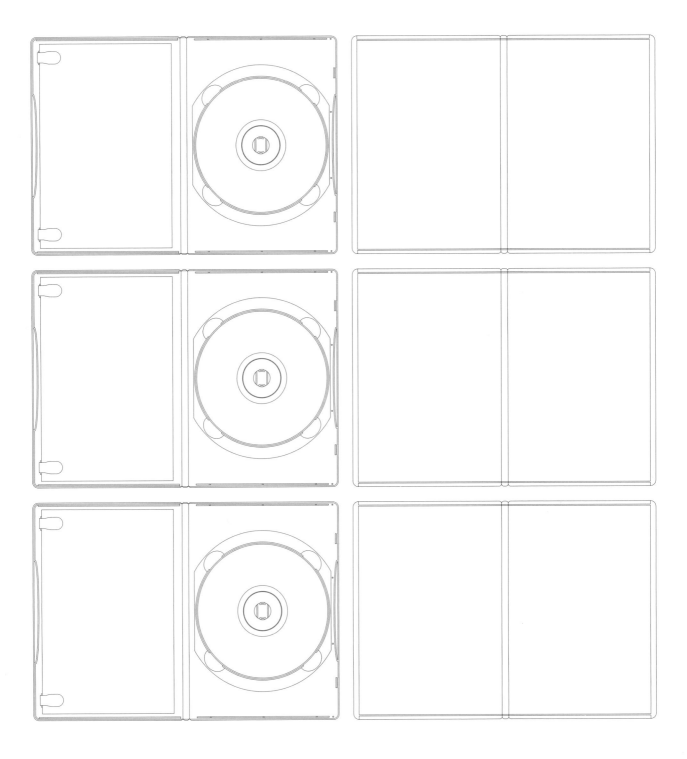

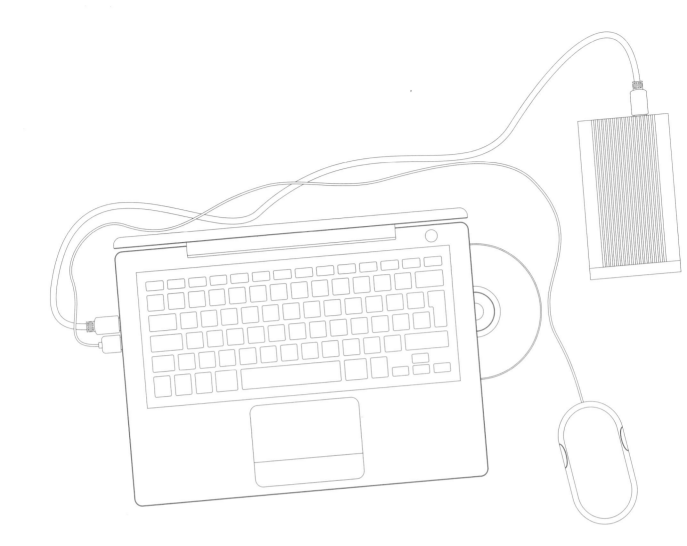
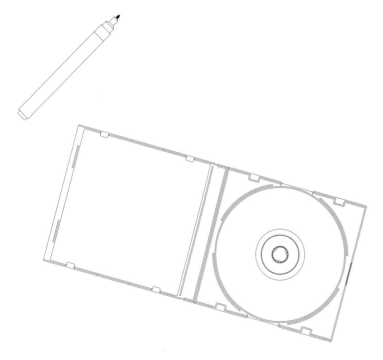

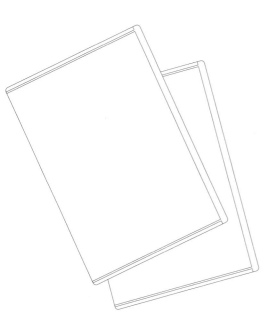

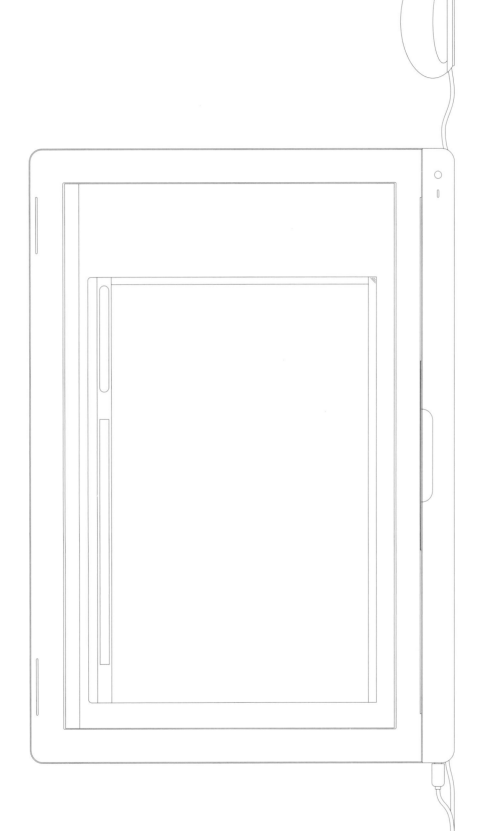

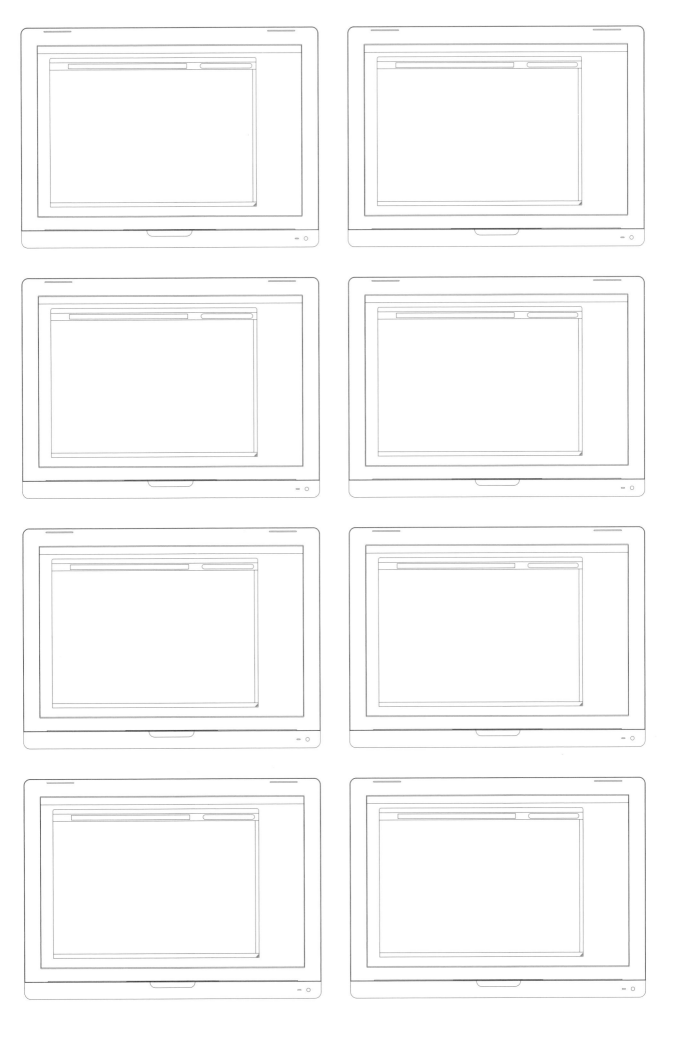

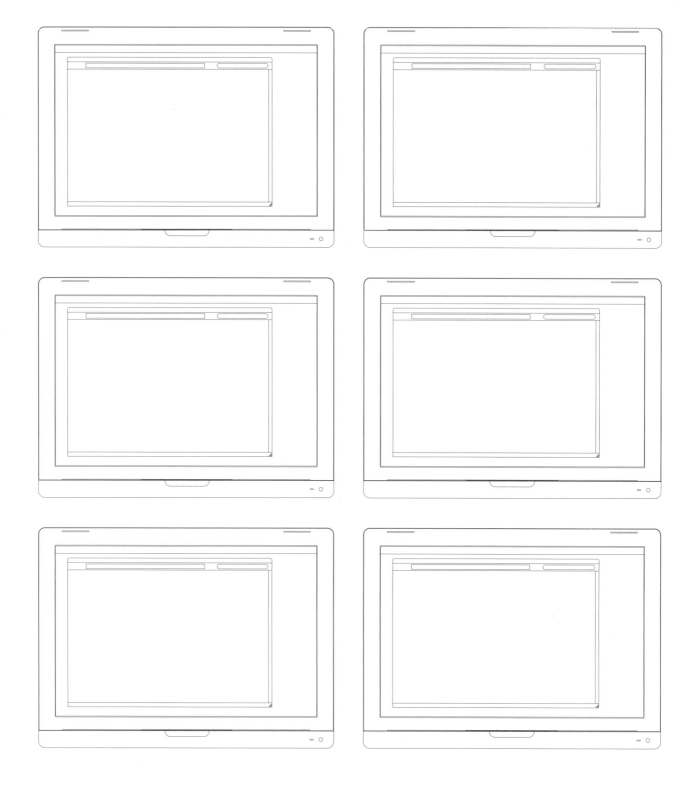

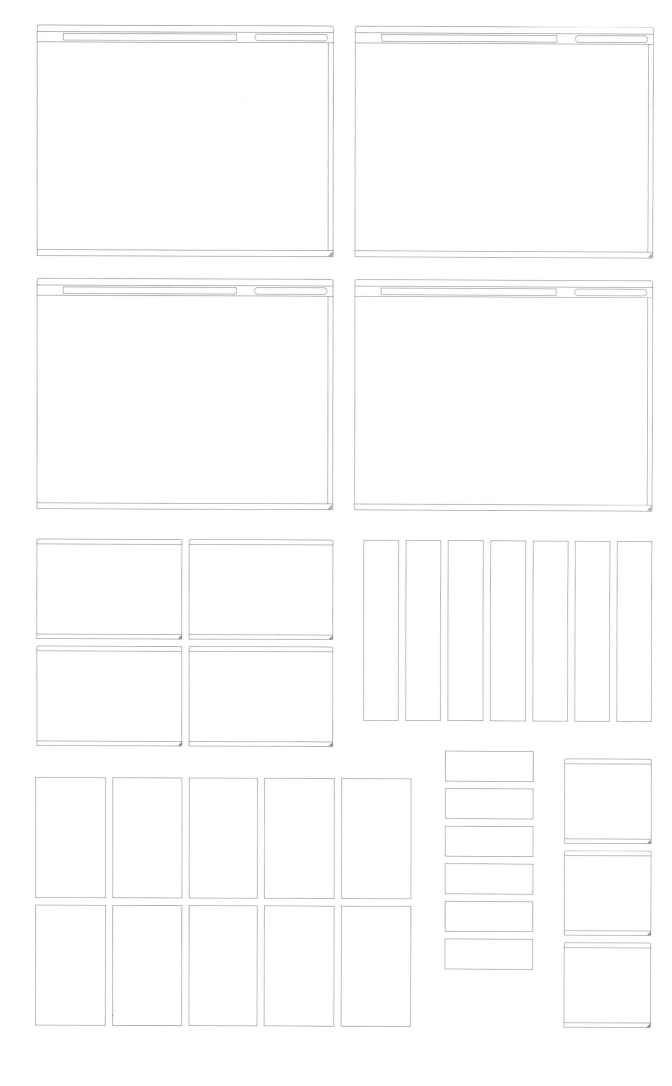

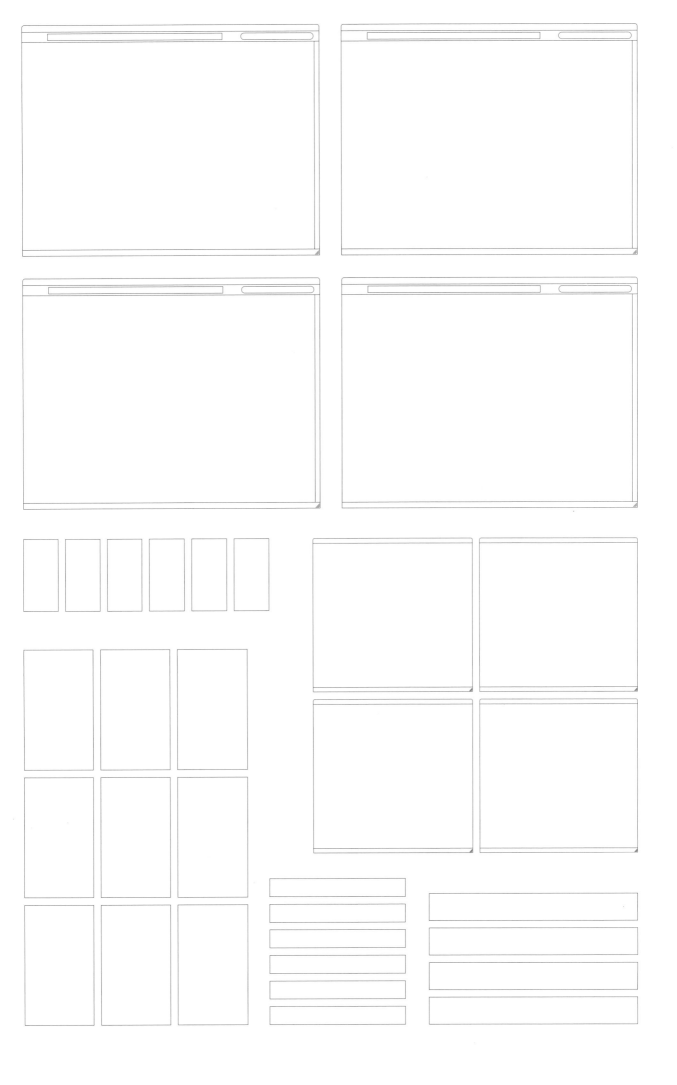

Sizes May Vary

Thumbnail/disc index
Item/page/file

Paper
International standards

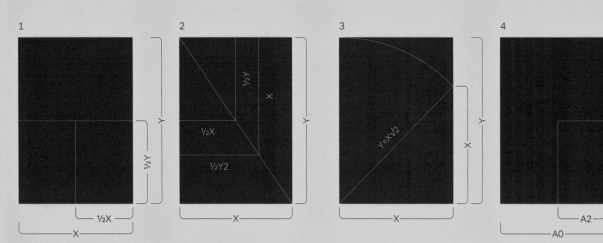

The international standard for paper sizing is the ISO* system. This system consists of three trimmed and two untrimmed series. The trimmed series are known as A (main), B (subsidiary), and C (intermediate); the untrimmed as R (raw), and SR (supplementary raw). The ISO system uses the metric unit of measurement and is accepted as standard in most countries, excluding the United States and Canada. The various sizes in this system are constructed from the base size of the A series (A0), which has an area of $1m^2$. Successive sizes in each series are acquired by halving the long dimension, or by doubling the shortest (1). All sizes are geometrically similar to one another (2) and have a height to width ratio of the square root of 2 (3). Each size in a series is represented by a letter and a number (4). The number represents how many times the base size (always zero) has been divided. For larger sizes, a prefix is added, which represents how many times the base size has been multiplied. The B series is acquired by calculating the geometric mean of successive A sizes; and the C series by calculating the geometric means between corresponding A and B sizes (5). A variation of these standards is the JIS B series used only in Japan. Fractionally larger than its ISO equivalent, this series of sizes is acquired by calculating the arithmetic mean of successive A sizes. The RA and SRA series are untrimmed raw paper. These formats are slightly larger than the corresponding A series and will be trimmed to size after printing and binding. The RA series allows for 5% of waste and the SRA series 15%.

*To prevent the use of different abbreviations in different languages the International Organization for Standardization uses a language independent word. This word is derived from the Greek, "isos" meaning "equal". Subsequently, the short form of the organization's name is always ISO.

Paper
International standards

A series (mm)

4A0	1682	2378
2A0	1189	1682
A0	841	1189
A1	594	841
A2	420	594
A3	297	420
A4	210	297
A5	148	210
A6	105	148
A7	74	105
A8	52	74
A9	37	52
A10	26	37

B series (mm)

B0	1000	1414
B1	707	1000
B2	500	707
B3	353	500
B4	250	353
B5	176	250
B6	125	176
B7	88	125
B8	62	88
B9	44	62
B10	31	44

JIS B series (mm)

B0	1030	1456
B1	728	1030
B2	515	728
B3	364	515
B4	257	364
B5	182	257
B6	128	182
B7	91	128
B8	64	91
B9	45	64
B10	32	45

A1 · A5 · A4 · A9 · A8 · A6 · A7 · A2 · A3

A0 (1m²)

C series (mm)

C0	917	1297
C1	648	917
C2	458	648
C3	324	458
C4	229	324
C5	162	229
C6	114	162
C7	81	114
C8	57	81

RA series (mm)

RA0	860	1220
RA1	610	860
RA2	430	610
RA3	305	420
RA4	215	305

SRA series (mm)

SRA0	900	1280
SRA1	640	900
SRA2	450	640
SRA3	320	450
SRA4	225	320

6

- ⅛A4
- ¼A4
- ⅓A4
- DL

Long sizes (mm)

⅛A4	13	210
¼A4	74	210
⅓A4	99	210

The proportions of the A series are often modified to suit other applications; the standard name for these modifications is long sizes. Long sizes are achieved by dividing the long dimension by three, four or eight equal parts (6). The most commonly used long size is ⅓A4, which fits without folding into a DL format envelope. Long sizes are classified by placing a fraction before their name. The beauty of the international system is that it allows for easy scaling* from one size to another (7). This functionality means that no information is lost and less paper is wasted. The majority of photocopiers outside of North America have preset functions that enable enlargements from A4 to A3 (141%) and reductions from A3 to A4 (71%).

7

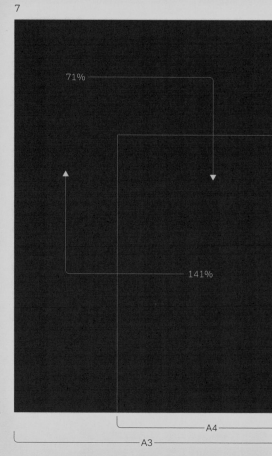

71%

141%

A4

A3

A series scaling %

	A0	A1	A2	A3	A4	A5	A6	A7	A8	A9	A10
A0	100	71	50	35	25	18	12.5	8.8	6.2	4.4	3.1
A1	141	100	71	50	35	25	18	12.5	8.8	6.2	4.4
A2	200	141	100	71	50	35	25	18	12.5	8.8	6.2
A3	283	200	141	100	71	50	35	25	18	12.5	8.8
A4	400	283	200	141	100	71	50	35	25	18	12.5
A5	566	400	283	200	141	100	71	50	35	25	18
A6	800	566	400	283	200	141	100	71	50	35	25
A7	1131	800	566	400	283	200	141	100	71	50	35
A8	1600	1131	800	566	400	283	200	141	100	71	50
A9	2263	1600	1131	800	566	400	283	200	141	100	71
A10	3200	2263	1600	1131	800	566	400	283	200	141	100

*Technical drawing pens follow the same scaling principles as international paper. Standard sizes in a series are in the ratio 2:1; therefore drawing with a 0.35mm pen on A3 paper and reducing it to A4, you can continue with the 0.25mm pen.

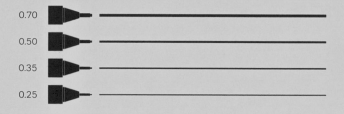

0.70

0.50

0.35

0.25

Paper
International standards

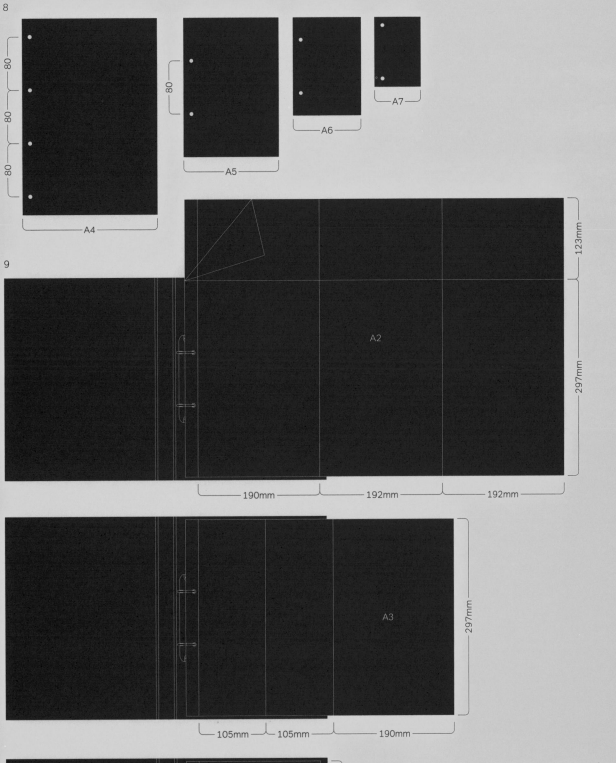

80
80
80

A4

80

A5

A6

A7

123mm

A2

297mm

190mm — 192mm — 192mm

A3

297mm

105mm — 105mm — 190mm

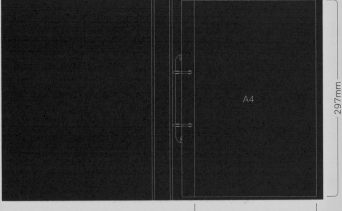

A4

297mm

190mm

There is also an international standard for the dimension and location of filing holes in paper (8). This system can be used to file any paper size larger than A7. A four-hole extension is also widely used (although not standardized) which is sometimes referred to as the "888" system, due to the 8cm gaps between each hole. A standard method for folding A series sheets to A4 format for filing also exists (9). This technique ensures that a 20mm single-layer margin for filing holes remains. The page can then be unfolded and folded again without being removed from the file.

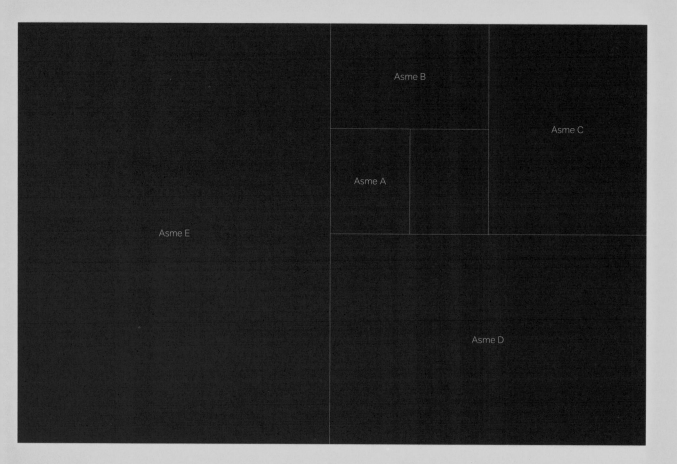

Traditional/Asme (in)

Invoice	-	5½	8½
Executive	-	7¼	10½
Letter	Asme A	8½	11
Legal	-	8½	14
Tabloid	Asme B	11	17
Broadsheet	Asme C	17	22
Cover	-	20	26
-	Asme D	22	34
Newsprint	-	24	36
Book/text	-	25	38
-	Asme E	34	44
-	Asme F	48	28

P series (mm)

P1	560	860
P2	430	560
P3	280	430
P4	215	280
P5	140	215
P6	107	140

The American national standard for paper sizing is the ASME* system, which defines decimal inch sheet sizes and formats. The majority of the sizes in this system are based on multiplications of the A size, which has the same dimensions as traditional US letter paper (8½ x 11 inches). This system also includes roll formats that are based on increments of 8½ or 11 inch segments. Unlike the ISO system, the dimensions of the base size (A) forces this standard to have two alternating aspect ratios. The national standard for Canada is the P Series. This series of sizes is based on ASME formats, but with all dimensions rounded to metric measurements. In addition to these standards, both the United States and Canada use traditional paper sizes (some listed) and a wide variety of specialist formats.

*The American Society of Mechanical Engineers is a standards developing organization that processes and maintains codes and standards for the American National Standards Institute. Standards developed under this program are often designated as ANSI or ANSI/ASME.

Envelopes
International standards

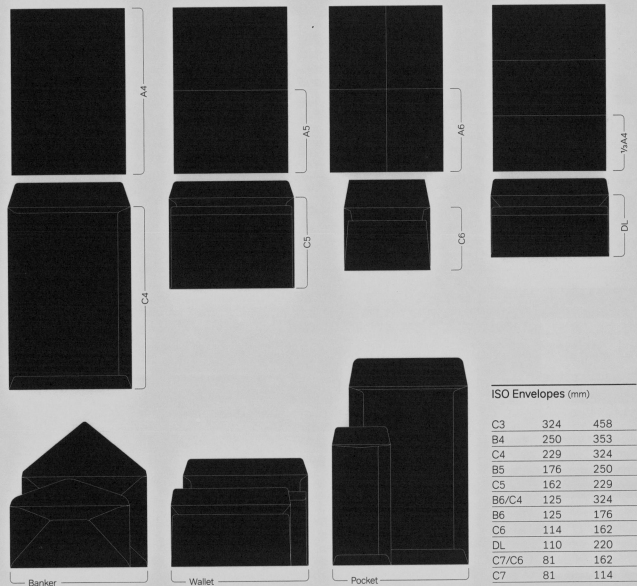

ISO Envelopes (mm)

C3	324	458
B4	250	353
C4	229	324
B5	176	250
C5	162	229
B6/C4	125	324
B6	125	176
C6	114	162
DL	110	220
C7/C6	81	162
C7	81	114

Designed to hold international paper sizes, standard ISO envelopes are a combination of B and C series sizes plus the introduction of a new format now known as DL (dimension lengthwise). Standard envelopes are ordinarily manufactured in three main styles: Banker, Wallet, and Pocket. Banker and Wallet envelopes have an opening/flap on the long side; Pocket envelopes on the short side. As with ISO paper sizes, Japan has its own variant to these standards. Standard JIS (Japanese Industrial Standard) envelopes have evolved from metricated traditional sizes and are also produced in three main styles.

JIS Envelopes (mm)

Rectangular No 2	119	277
Rectangular No 3	120	235
Rectangular No 4	90	205
Rectangular No 40	90	225
Square No 0	287	382
Square No 2	240	332
Square No 20/C4	229	324
Square No 3	216	277
Square No 4	197	267
Square No 5	190	240
Square No 6/C5	162	229
Square No 7	142	205
Square No 8	119	197
Western No 1	120	176
Western No 2/C6	114	162
Western No 4	105	235
Western No 6	98	190

Envelopes
North American standards

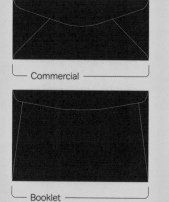
Commercial

Booklet

Wallet

Window

Catalog

Standard North American envelopes are divided into several categories—by their style and their function. Each category has its own range of sizes.

Announcement

Remittance

Policy

Baronial

Commercial (in)

No 5	3⅛	5½
No 6	3⅜	6
No 6¼	3½	6
No 6¾	3⅝	6½
No 7	3¾	6¾
Monarch No 7¾	3⅞	7½
Data Card Check	3½	7⅝
No 8⅝	3⅝	8⅝
No 9	3⅞	8⅞
No 10	4⅛	9½
No 10½	4½	9½
No 11	4½	10⅜
No 12	4¾	11
No 14	5	11½

Booklet (in)

No 2½	4½	5⅞
No 3	4¾	6½
No 4¼	5	7½
No 5	5½	8⅛
No 6	5¾	8⅞
No 6½	6	9
No 6¾	6½	9½
No 7¼	7	10
No 7½	7½	10½
No 8	8	11⅛
No 9	8¾	11½
No 9½	9	12
No 10	9½	12⅝
No 13	10	13

Wallet (in)

No 10	4⅛	9½
No 11	4½	10⅜
No 12	4¾	11
No 14	5	11½

Window (in)*

No 6¼	3½	6
No 6¾	3⅝	6½
No 7	3¾	6¾
No 7¾	3⅞	7½
No 8⅝	3⅝	8⅝
No 9	3⅞	8⅞
No 10	4⅛	9½
No 11	4½	10⅜
No 14	5	11½

Catalog (in)

No 1	6	9
No 1¾	6½	9½
No 3	7	10
No 6	7½	10½
No 8	8¼	11¼
No 9½	8½	11½
No 9¾	8¾	11¼
No 10½	9	12
No 12½	9½	12½
No 13½	10	13
No 14½	11½	14½

Announcement (in)

A 2	4⅜	5¾
A 6	4¾	6½
A 7	5¼	7¼
A 8	5½	8⅛
A 10	6	9½
Slim/long	3⅞	8⅞

Remittance (in)

No 6¼	3½	6
No 6½	3½	6¼
No 6¾	3⅝	6½
No 9	3⅞	8⅞

Policy (in)

9	4	9
10	4⅛	9½
11	4½	10⅜
12	4¾	11
14	5	11½

Baronial (in)

Gladstone	3⁹⁄₁₆	5⁹⁄₁₆
No 4	3⅝	5⅛
No 5	4⅛	5½
No 5¼	4¼	5¼
53	4⅛	6¼
No 5½	4⅜	5¾
No 6	4¾	6½
110	5	7¼
Lee	5¼	7¼
137	5½	8½

*The standard window size is 4½ in wide by 1⅛ in deep and positioned ⅞ in away from the left edge and ⅝ in above the bottom edge. For No 8⅝ format the position is ¾ in from the left and 1³⁄₁₆ in from the bottom.

Outdoor formats
International

Posters and billboards (mm)

4 sheet	1016	1524
12 sheet	3048	1524
16 sheet	2032	3048
32 sheet	4064	3048
48 sheet	6096	3048
64 sheet	8128	3048
96 sheet	12192	3048
6 sheet	1200	1800

The outdoor advertising industry in the UK, and a large percentage of the international market, use the 4-sheet poster system (10). The 4-sheet gets its name from the 60- by 40-inch double quad crown posters used on the London underground in the 1920s. This format was four times the size of the double crown that measured 30 by 20 inches. Traditionally, 4-sheet posters are printed onto blue-backed poster paper and pasted up singly or in multiples to create larger sizes. Today, these larger sizes are also printed as one sheet and back-lit in huge lightboxes. Another standard format is the 6-sheet poster (11), which is roughly 6 times larger than the traditional double crown. 6-sheets are used throughout Europe and Asia, illuminated on bus shelters and stand-alone ad shells.

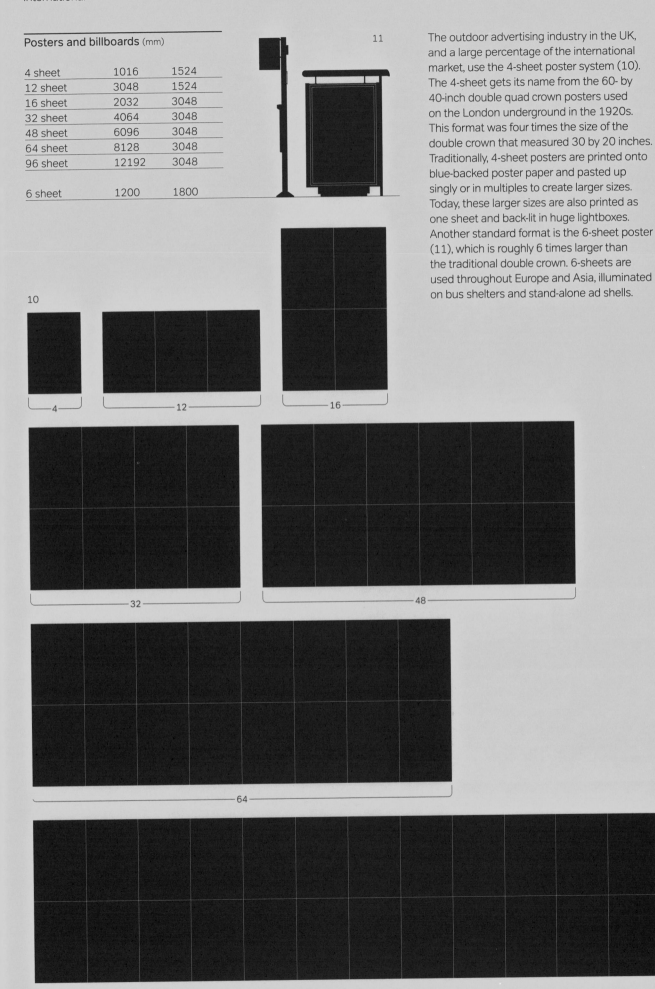

In addition to 4- and 6-sheet posters and billboards (page 315), many international countries also specify their own unique range of outdoor advertising formats.

Germany (mm)

4/1	1185	1750
6/1	1190	2520
8/1	1190	3360
18/1	3560	2520

UK (mm)

Double Crown	508	762
Quad Crown	762	1016
Double Royal	635	1016
Double Quad	1016	1524
200's	3000	6000
Square	3000	3000
250's	4500	3000
Square	6000	6000
450's	7500	5000
500's	4500	9000
1000's	4600	18000

Australia (mm)

Bus shelter	1200	1800
6 sheet	3000	1500
24 sheet	6100	3000
Supersite	12660	3350

France (mm)

2 m²	1185	1750
8 m²	3200	2400
12 m²	4000	3000

Spain (mm)

Urbano	1185	1750
4x3	4000	3000
8x3	8000	3000

Italy (mm)

Telefono/Bus	100	140
Stendardi	1400	2000
Senior	3200	2400
4x3	4000	3000
6x3	6000	3000
6x6	6000	6000

Switzerland (mm)

F4	895	1280
F200	1190	1700
F12	2685	1280
F24	2685	2560
GF	3980	2950

Netherlands (mm)

Abri	1185	1750
Billboard	3400	2440

North America has several standardized formats for outdoor advertising. These range from illuminated transit shelters and 8- or 30-sheet posters found in residential and commercial areas, to large super-sized bulletin billboards located on major freeways. 8- and 30-sheet posters are produced in several finished formats, printed to bleed or wrapped, square or round corners, and in some areas, poster boards are stacked, one on top of the other, creating a larger surface area.

Posters and billboards (ft/in)

Transit shelter	68½	47½
8 sheet (round corner)	5' 4	11' 4
8 sheet (wrapped)	6' 2	12' 2
30 sheet (standard)	9' 7	21' 7
30 sheet (bleed)	10' 5	22' 8
30 sheet (wrapped)	12' 3	24' 6
30 sheet (stacked/square)	24' 6	24' 6
Bulletin	10' 6	36'
-	10'	40'
-	14'	48'
Super bulletin	16'	60'
-	20'	60'

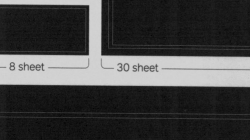

8 sheet — 30 sheet

Bulletins

Super bulletins

Digital formats
Audio/video and data discs

The CD and DVD are the most common formats for the storage and distribution of video, audio, and digital data. Developed jointly by Philips and Sony in 1982, the CD or compact disc is 1.2mm thick and has a diameter of 120mm. A CD can hold approximately 74–80 minutes of audio or 650–700 megabytes of data. The dimensions of a DVD are the same, but a standard DVD can store up to 4.7 gigabytes, whereas variants of dual layer and double sided hold from 8.5–15.9 gigabytes. Many variations of packaging have been developed for both types of disc, the most consistent being the jewel case and the keep case.

Sleeve

124mm

125, 125mm

16, 125, 16mm

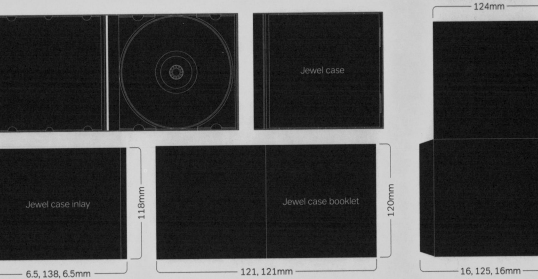

Jewel case

Jewel case inlay

118mm

6.5, 138, 6.5mm

Jewel case booklet

120mm

121, 121mm

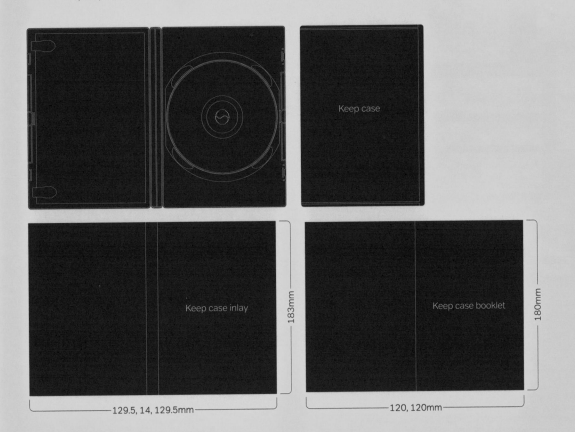

Keep case

Keep case inlay

183mm

129.5, 14, 129.5mm

Keep case booklet

180mm

120, 120mm

Digital formats
Browsers/banners and pop-ups

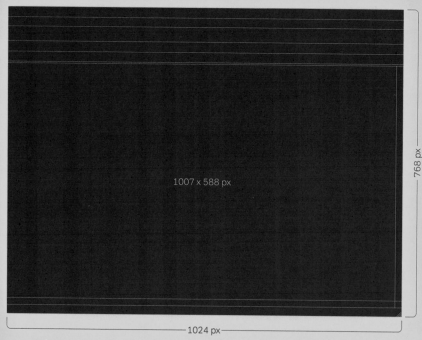

12

1007 x 588 px

768 px

1024 px

Statistically, the most common screen resolution used by browsers of the World Wide Web is 1024 x 768 pixels or more. Taking into account the different types of operating systems, and the browser chrome* associated with each of the different applications used, this visual area (12) is reduced to approximately 1007 x 588. The IAB (International Advertising Bureau) has sought to introduce several standard sizes for advertising on the World Wide Web. These standards (13) are "intended for marketers, agencies, and media companies for use in the creating, planning, buying, and selling of interactive marketing and advertising." Although not standardized, these guidelines provide a framework for the vast majority of online advertising.

13

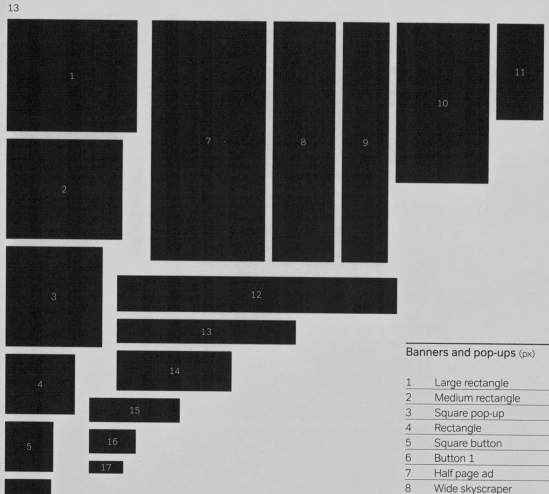

*Browser chrome is the graphical framework and elements of a web browser. Common elements include the title bar and toolbar, the horizontal and vertical scrollbars, and the status bar.

Banners and pop-ups (px)

1	Large rectangle	336	280
2	Medium rectangle	300	250
3	Square pop-up	250	250
4	Rectangle	180	150
5	Square button	125	125
6	Button 1	120	90
7	Half page ad	300	600
8	Wide skyscraper	160	600
9	Skyscraper	120	600
10	Vertical rectangle	240	400
11	Vertical banner	120	240
12	Leaderboard	728	90
13	Full banner	468	60
14	3:1 rectangle	300	100
15	Half banner	234	60
16	Button 2	120	60
17	Micro bar	88	31

Measures
Millimeters/inches/picas and points

25.4 millimeters (mm) = 1inch (in)
1in = 72 postscript point* (pt)
72pt = 6 pica (p)

mm – in	
1	0.039
2	0.079
3	0.118
4	0.157
5	0.197
6	0.236
7	0.276
8	0.315
9	0.354
10	0.394
11	0.433
12	0.472
13	0.512
14	0.551
15	0.591
16	0.630
17	0.669
18	0.709
19	0.748
20	0.787
30	1.181
40	1.575
50	1.969
60	2.362
70	2.756
80	3.150
90	3.543
100	3.937

pt – mm	
6	2.116
7	2.469
8	2.822
9	3.175
10	3.527
11	3.88
12	4.23
14	4.938
18	6.35
24	8.46
30	10.583
36	12.7
48	16.933
60	21.166
72	25.4

in – mm	
0.25	6.35
0.5	12.7
0.75	19.1
1	25.4
1.5	38.1
2	50.8
2.5	63.5
3	76.2
3.5	88.9
4	101.6
4.5	114.3
5	127
5.5	139.7
6	152.4
6.5	165.1
7	177.8
7.5	190.5
8	203.2
8.5	215.9
9	228.6
9.5	241.3
10	254

*The postscript point is the most popular unit of typographical measurement. It has largely surpassed the traditional typesetter's point, which varied in size by continent. The French, European Didot point is 0.148in, and the Anglo-American point is 0.13837in. Adobe rounded this measurement to 0.014in (72 per inch) with the invention of the postscript language.

Millimeter	Inch	Pica	Point
10			
20	1	6	72
30			
40			
50	2	12	144
60			
70			
80	3	18	216
90			
100	4	24	288
110			
120			
130	5	30	360
140			
150	6	36	432
160			
170			
180	7	42	504
190			
200	8	48	576
210			
220			
230	9	54	648
240			
250	10	60	720
260			
270			

Referenced standards: ISO 216, Writing paper and certain classes of
printed matter—Trimmed sizes—A and B series. JIS P 0138, Writing
paper and certain classes of printed matter—Trimmed sizes—A and B
series. ISO 217, Paper—Untrimmed sizes—Designation and tolerances
for primary and supplementary ranges, and indication of machine
direction. ISO 838, Paper—Holes for general filing purposes. DIN 824,
Technical drawings—Folding to filing size. ASME Y14.1, Decimal inch
drawing sheet size and format. CAN/CGSB 9.60 94, Paper sizes for
correspondence. ISO 269, Correspondence envelopes—Designation
and sizes. JIS S 5502, Envelopes and pockets.